INTELLIGENT
BUSINESS
ALLIANCES

INTELLIGENT BUSINESS ALLIANCES

HOW TO PROFIT

USING TODAY'S

MOST IMPORTANT

STRATEGIC TOOL

Larraine Segil

Partner and Co-Founder, The Lared Group

TIMES BUSINESS

RANDOM HOUSE

Library of Congress Cataloging-in-Publication Data

Segil, Larraine.
    Intelligent business alliances : how to profit using today's most important strategic tool / Larraine D. Segil. — 1st ed.
        p.   cm.
    Includes bibliographical references and index.
    ISBN 0-8129-2466-5
    1. Strategic alliances (Business)   I. Title.
HD69.S8S44   1996
658'.044—dc20   95-49794

Random House website address: http://www.randomhouse.com/
Printed in the United States of America on acid-free paper
9 8 7

Designed by Levavi & Levavi

I dedicate this book to my sister,
Pamela Goldberg, whose love and friendship
transcends time and distance
and is always with me.

Acknowledgments

I thank my incredibly supportive husband, Clive Segil. This book is the result of thousands of hours of research, writing, and reviewing—most of which were taken from nights, weekends, and vacations, time that he and I would have spent together. Equally influential and meaningful were the intuitive comments and clarity of thought that came from my son, James, a young rising international executive who has always taken time from his schedule to give me input.

The balancing act of working on this book, juggling responsibilities at The Lared Group, and satisfying my drive to get a particular insight or thought into the manuscript was greatly supported by my partner of ten years, Emilio Fontana. Many of the real-life examples that I use in the book are illustrations from cases that Emilio and I have experienced first hand in consulting with organizations worldwide on how to strategize and create and manage strategic alliances. I thank him for being a great partner, for his insights and contributions to our joint endeavors in The Lared Group, and for many of the shared experiences on which I draw extensively in this book.

Many hours of work and follow-up have gone into the charts, diagrams, and figures that make up an important part of this book. All of them were crafted by Flo Dunagan, our tireless assistant at The Lared Group. She has provided invaluable support, expertise in innumerable software programs, and general energy and good humor for the ten years that she has organized activities at The Lared Group. Flo, my heartfelt thanks.

Gwen Uman, founder of Comp.U.Stat, had the statistical brainpower that took my data and made sense of it all. Thanks, Gwen, for a superb and professional job. Beth Kinsolving was an active contributor to the early stages of data collation; thanks for your assistance.

Gaylord Nick Nickols, executive director of the Industrial Relations Center at the California Institute of Technology, has been an enthusiastic fan; he provided me with a forum for making presentations. I gain enormous pleasure and am fired with delight and energy whenever I'm offered a chance to give a speech, run a seminar, or develop a lively discussion. Nick, thanks for letting me do what I love! It is owing to the Center's amazing staff—Anne Campbell, Delores Lee, Toni Parhizgar, Anne Marie Simoneau, Bettye Dilworth, Pamela Haynes, Miki Kumamoto, and Wendy Magallanes—that I can enjoy my seminars so much. Thank you all for your support and professionalism. My gratitude to Barbara Huff-Duff, librarian extraordinaire! A special thanks to Sue Lewis.

Andrew Galef, Chairman and CEO of MagneTek, and Lloyd Cotsen, former CEO of Neutrogena, have contributed to this book with their feedback and advice—I thank you both.

The many hundreds of executives who have participated in my survey gave generously of their time and insights. I promised you all that I'd share the results with the world and still keep your names confidential, and I've kept to that commitment. Thank you for your assistance.

Elaine Markson and Sarah Flynn, your support and expertise have been my impetus when the workload became overwhelming. Thanks for letting me rely on you both to accomplish what you do so well.

My editor, Karl Weber, and the wonderful Times Business team, your professionalism makes me look good and I thank you all.

I have met many in my business life who have given me cause to ponder and ultimately create the Mindshift approach. I thank you all for helping me mature in my understanding of business and human nature.

Foreword

When a business book challenges readers to reexamine their day-to-day operations with a newer awareness and provides a set of solutions that work, the time spent in reading it becomes an investment that can be leveraged over a lifetime. Larraine Segil's *Intelligent Business Alliances* is such a book. Larraine Segil has created an approach to alliances that brings clarity and specific analytical tools to the complex world of the interrelationship of organizations.

In the past several decades, many organizations have developed alliance relationships locally, nationally, and internationally, in varying combinations. Many of these alliances have been pursued for sound business reasons; others have not. Too often, the costs of a failed alliance far exceed the capital invested; the negative impact can be felt in jobs lost, technology unwittingly transferred, and competitive advantages yielded.

My experience in the commercialization of technology and the establishment of over one hundred viable technology companies that employ tens of thousands of people and generate many billions of dollars both domestically and worldwide has shown me that well-designed alliances have a multiplier effect on local and national economies. Segil's method of analyzing alliances and interorganizational relationships is a substantive and critical tool for present and future managers that will enable them to achieve a higher level of success in the alliance process, in technology-based organizations and in many other arenas as well.

As cofounder of Teledyne, Inc., I was privileged, as that company grew and diversified, to work with many of the corporate, managerial, and project personality types mentioned in this book.

I have seen the life-cycle process that Segil describes here so vividly, repeated in every organization with which I have been associated. It also applies to the nonprofits that I have helped create, such as IC2 (the Institute of Innovation, Creativity and Capital), the Austin Technology Incubator (offering help and facilities for start-up firms), the Texas Capital Network (a group of business "angels" who provide risk capital to entrepreneurs), and the Institute of Management Sciences, as well as educational institutions to which I've had the opportunity to contribute, such as the University of Texas at Austin, where I was dean of the College and Graduate School of Business Administration.

Readers who are already experienced in alliances will absorb this text, dramatically change their minds about the concept of corporate and managerial personality, and be forced into a broader appreciation of domestic and international alliance relationships by the fascinating view into the future that Segil provides, as she synthesizes a multitude of significant perspectives.

The novice alliance manager will find it difficult to put down this thought-provoking, easy-to-read book. Its logical, systematic approach to alliance strategy, structure, and implementation provides a guide that will become the standard for all managers who delve into this challenging area, since it is practical and mind-stretching at the same time.

Alliances challenge even the most expert manager. Understanding how to make alliances work better will become an important competitive management talent, in demand by organizations worldwide. This book makes a major contribution to the transformation of alliances into a new and basic functional area for corporate management.

—Dr. George Kozmetsky,
Cofounder, Teledyne, Inc.

Contents

Contents
xii

List of Cases

Introduction

It was a simple distribution arrangement: One company would sell the products of the other. The contract was signed—and then the problems began. A sales commission issue arose; it took four committee meetings over seven months before a decision maker in Jenson Aerospace* would act. At Maxwell Electronics,* the frustration of the division manager grew. Tempers flared and trust began to fracture. Then a competitor started moving strongly into the target market. A quick response was called for, but was it possible for these two partners to act quickly? The next meeting between managers of the two companies was heated.

"What is wrong with you guys? Does every decision have to be treated like a federal case? Can't you see we're losing the market while you twiddle your thumbs in meetings?"

"You don't understand. We have processes here. We can't just jump into things—we take our time to look at options and make a careful decision. You should have known this is how we operate. This deal was structured the way your CEO wanted it—don't complain about it now."

"Well, our CEO never asked me. And now the relationship is falling apart because you people take forever to move on problems. Isn't there someone who'll make a decision in your organization?"

Four months later, someone did. The relationship was dissolved because of "incompatibility of goals"—at least, that's how the brief press release phrased it.

There were conflicts on many levels of this relationship. Unfortunately, miscommunications and misunderstandings that under-

---

* Names have been changed.

mine and destroy business alliances are all too frequent. The purpose of this book is to provide you with the tools to anticipate and thus plan to avoid or manage some of the problems that make many business alliances fail. The most important of these tools is the Mindshift approach, a new language and way of looking at business relationships. The Mindshift tools of personality diagnosis will help you see yourself, your own organization, and your present or potential business partners in a new, highly revealing light.

This book is for CEOs, middle managers, and staff members of both large and small companies. It is designed to be useful for entrepreneurs as well as for leaders of nonprofit organizations. Anyone from the board of directors to a management trainee can benefit from understanding the philosophy, process, and methodology you'll be learning.

In today's global environment, technology is eroding the control of nations over knowledge on the basis of national borders and accelerating the speed of change. As a result, domestic and cross-cultural business alliances are becoming a competitive necessity—not just the latest management fad. For many companies, alliances are the most expedient way to obtain knowledge, market access, and strategic growth.

But relationships between organizations, whether small or large, for profit or not-for-profit, are complex and demand management's finest skills. Practical issues, interpersonal dynamics, and external market stressors can add complications to even the simplest business partnership.

The failure statistics regarding business alliances are disheartening. Professor Kathryn Rudie Harrigan of Columbia University has discovered that 55 percent of all strategic alliances fall apart within three to five years of inception. In her cross-industry sample, the remaining 45 percent, the ones that were considered successful, had a further life expectancy of just 3.5 years.[1] We have to find ways to develop and manage these relationships that will ensure a better success rate.

The key lies in the processes used to understand our own businesses and create alliances with others. Recognizing what drives your company, motivates your managers, and creates successful projects for you is a threshold requirement for the development of effective partnerships with others.

My career has required me to develop a variety of management skills—cross-cultural, entrepreneurial, and operational. I've been involved in both domestic and international business, first as a lawyer, then as an operator of four businesses I cofounded.

My experience as CEO of a distribution company for advanced materials sold to the aerospace and electronics markets threw me headlong into the alliance field. As a small company, we relied on alliances with larger organizations, and my challenge was to make enough noise for us to be noticed in the hierarchy of a complex big-company bureaucracy. It was then that I realized the importance of project priority in alliances as well as the limiting factors of contrasting corporate and managerial personalities. These were the real issues that I faced every day. Product distribution was the easy part; overcoming the personality dynamics was the major challenge.

Personality issues in business are intriguing; they add a human dimension to management theory. I've found that the personality characteristics of managers, their projects, and their organizations are simple to identify. The hard part is to integrate the information into a planning and implementation methodology to manage your business and create better alliances. The honesty, will, and tenacity needed to bring about the sometimes painful structural and organizational changes that may be called for does not come easily to most businesses.

Over the past ten years, as alliances have become more popular, many experts have proposed different structures to help alliance relationships succeed—negotiated terms of agreement, options, escape clauses, and other business and legal devices. Structural considerations can be important. But if the decision-making process used and the personalities of the implementers, both individual and organizational, don't mesh and cannot work together in harmony and with mutuality, the project may well be doomed to failure, no matter what its legal structure.

Your organization may not have the optimum personality characteristics to succeed in a particular alliance. Finding that out before entering into a complicated, time-consuming, costly relationship could be the best investment of time and effort you'll make. The Mindshift system will help you make that determination, leading to more realistic expectations and a higher probability of a success in the alliances you choose to enter.

The case histories in this book, often disguised, are taken from twelve years of experience with alliances by our consulting firm, The Lared Group, as well as by my own companies. The recommendations made are based on this experience and the results of the Mindshift survey of 235 companies from many different industries, which yielded important information on how alliances work—or don't work—in real-life business. Our method will give you a deeper understanding of the potential pitfalls caused by a disharmony of corporate and individual belief systems and cultures or by divergent corporate structures and methodology. It should allow you to enter a possibly risky alliance with your eyes opened to the difficulties ahead—or perhaps to avoid such an alliance altogether.

Structure of the Book

Most readers want to get to the bottom line in a business book quickly. Here is the structure of this one.

Chapter 1, "Alliances Revisited," defines alliances for the purposes of this book and explains the nature and importance of business alliances that are well managed as opposed to those alliances that reflect only a fad.

Chapter 2, "The Mindshift Method of Personality Diagnostics" presents the core of the approach.* This method enables you to analyze and understand various kinds of business personalities—corporate, individual managerial, and project—and relates them to the life cycles of organizations.

Chapter 3, "Integrating Alliances into Corporate Strategy," tells how to make your alliance strategy an effective, coherent element in the overall growth plan for your organization.

Chapter 4, "Corporate Self-Analysis," examines the critical internal study that must take place prior to entering into alliance activities, as a prerequisite to performing a balanced evaluation of partner candidates.

Chapter 5, "Preparing for the Alliance," explains how to plan an alliance and how to manage the partner search and selection process from initial talks until the deal is closed.

Chapter 6, "Cross-Cultural Alliances," addresses the issues that arise in international alliances and that overlay and often complicate the decisions covered in Chapter 3.

Chapter 7, "Implementing and Managing the Alliance," considers the partnership as a continuing process that begins with alliance planning and lasts for the lifetime of the alliance. You may already be involved in a business relationship that is less than perfect; this chapter will give you some insights into how to improve your ongoing partnerships.

Finally, Chapter 8, "A View of the Future World of Alliances," looks at some of the increasingly significant factors to be considered in the development of a macro approach to strategic alliances, including globalism, the virtual corporation, technology hybridization, and broad-based changes in communication technology.

Appendixes A, B, and C contain information on companies whose executives were surveyed as part of the program I present at the California Institute of Technology, Pasadena. These executives

---

* Mindshift is a service mark of Larraine Segil.

applied the Mindshift method to their alliance activities, and I then did research on the outcomes. The results of that research are reflected throughout the book, especially in Chapter 5, and are summarized in Appendix D.

Welcome, then, to an intriguing journey on which you will discover who you are as a manager or company, what you'd like to be, and whether you have the best chance of getting there through the complex, promising world of alliances.

INTELLIGENT
BUSINESS
ALLIANCES

1.
Alliances
Revisited

Stan Meridian, CEO of Stanford Products, Inc.,* was at his most forceful. His entire management team was present, gathered together from all over the world at a wooded retreat near Houston. The business had been in Stan's family for fifty years. He was the third generation to be at the helm, and at $500 million in annual revenues the organization was more complex than ever before. The organization was reeling from its latest series of restructurings. Changes in their industry with the arrival of a competitive technology had caused him to do what no other member of his family had considered, lay off hundreds of loyal workers. Morale was low, although expenses had finally come under control.

Over the previous few difficult years, Stan had pondered whether he'd made the right decisions, but now the company finally seemed to be in recovery. In the past, the family had controlled the organization with a small team of managers. Recently, however, Stan had

* Names have been changed.

instituted a different structure, including new divisions and lines of business. In addition, he had been reading and hearing a great deal about the alliances concept. It seemed like a cost-effective way to begin growing the company again. The time had come to focus on the positive. This was the theme of Stan's address to his assembled managers.

"Strategic alliances are the strategy that will propel our company into the new millennium. It is time for us to break out of the 'not invented here' culture that has demanded that we develop all technology in-house. The reason for the latest organizational change is to develop divisional responsibility, which gives each one of you the power to develop alliances that contribute to the strategic strength and direction of our company. It is time for us to recharacterize ourselves as a flexible, proactive, solutions-oriented company. I'm counting on you all."

Stan's message, in short: "Go thee forth and create a multitude of alliances."

Eighteen months later, Stan Meridian had achieved one of his goals: He had destroyed company inertia and improved morale. In place of these problems, however, the organization was wrestling with a plethora of conflicting opportunities. Many questions had arisen regarding the methodology of developing and managing alliances. Some of the key issues Stanford Products faced were the following:

- *Where is the appropriate place for decision-making authority regarding the selection of an alliance partner and of the team to manage the relationship?*
- *How should the organization sort out and define core company competencies?*
- *How should a team measure or quantify the success of an alliance?*
- *What is an intelligent strategy for resolving alliance conflicts without resorting to termination of the alliance or litigation?*

- *What is the role of the corporate director of alliances in relation to the members of operating management?*

None of these vital questions had clear answers. Obviously, Stanford Products had to revisit its approach to alliances.

The experience of Stanford Products is a common one. You may belong to an organization already in the throes of alliance development or operation. Whether you are experienced in alliance management or a novice, whether your company is the same size as Stan's, larger or smaller, public or private, the rule is the same: A company's ability to manage alliances will be established in the planning process. A well-planned alliance can be executed far more smoothly than one that is entered into in a reactive mode, as a response to an urgent partner who pushes strongly for deal closure or the orders of a CEO who has chosen alliances as the "strategy *du jour.*"

Failing to Plan = Planning to Fail

Recently, an executive of a major pharmaceuticals company told me about the extensive multimonth alliance-planning process her firm now engaged in long before approaching any potential partner. "We've learned by bitter experience," she explained. "The downside risks we've encountered by moving forward without this level of detailed planning have made us realize that the effort is essential.

"We have entered into four alliances over the past three years where planning was hasty. In one case, there was no plan at all—the partner approached us, a group of senior executives fell in love with the idea, and, with pressure for closure from the business-development people, whose main expertise had been focused on acquisitions, the contract was signed in six weeks.

"In all four cases, it was only after we were deep into the relationship that we discovered many of the problems that hampered our ability to succeed. For example, in one case, the team had not considered the criteria that would constitute success, and ways to measure them. We had no idea whether the project was meeting expectations or not. We simply kept funding it, with the target date for completion moving further and further into the future. We pulled out of that one just last month.

"Another alliance involved the creation of an autoimmune diagnostic product, where the regulatory approval process is far shorter than for some other pharmaceuticals. Our partner's way of making decisions was so circuitous that the window of opportunity was almost closed by the time the papers were ready for filing. We are now convinced that companies should get into the crucial alliance questions of *why, who, how,* and *when* sooner rather than later."

This book will cover many of the management problems that occur in established alliances. They begin with the partners' definition of what the alliance means to them. Differences in the definitions can mean that expectations are misaligned and disappointment inevitably follows. This threshold issue can be discovered in the planning process and may save your organization from making a costly mistake. Every chapter will illustrate the problems that occur in the established alliance when certain aspects of the planning process are inadequately followed. It is during planning, often long before the deal is signed or the alliance begins, that the seeds of a difficult relationship are planted.

Only those who are serious about the effort that ongoing alliances require will succeed. The fad of alliance creation has led to the use of the grand term "strategic alliance" for short-term, tactical, promotional, almost casual business arrangements. It's fun to speak of alliances—after all, everyone seems to be doing them. However, successful alliance relationships require commitment to problem resolution, a desire to learn as well as teach, and the application of genuine talent and meaningful resources. By applying the processes outlined in this book you will become familiar with the real risks and rewards of alliances and develop the skills to manage them better.

What Is an Alliance?

The term "alliance" can be applied to many kinds of relationships and is freely used in business, whether it is appropriate or not. Here is a plain definition of an alliance, as the term is used in this book:

An alliance is a relationship that is strategic or tactical, and that is entered into for mutual benefit by two or more parties having compatible or complementary business interests and goals.

Let's look at each part of the definition separately.

"Strategic"

The concepts "strategy" and "tactics" in business are overused and underexplained. The military definitions of strategy, tactics, and operations are just as valid in business and are helpful in clarifying important distinctions.

Strategy is the process of planning and directing operations into the most advantageous position before *entering into engagement.*

Tactics is the process of organizing during *engagement.*

Operations is the process of being *in action—the state of being actively involved in business activities and transactions.*

Strategy presumes a level of thoughtfulness, consideration, and concern about and planning for a changing future. Since tactics are techniques used during engagement, there is not as much time nor resources available for thinking, planning, and predicting. Tactical alliances are created in the midst of operations, without the careful thought and planning that would position the organization prior to entering into the business activity.

Operations are a series of ongoing business activities (e.g., taking orders, making sales, shipping products) that occur in the present, without much thought for the future. Unless operations are driven by strategy, they will continue in a direction set by past experience, not future opportunity. However, if an organization thinks about and designs a strategy, then operations can become the living implementation of that strategy.

In considering the future and change prediction that characterizes the concept of strategy, Henry Mintzberg, an eminent scholar of strategic management, defines the strategy-making process as

> capturing what the manager learns from all sources (both the soft insights from his or her personal experiences and the experiences of others throughout the organization and the hard data from market research and the like) and then synthesizing that learning into a vision of the direction that the business should pursue.[1]

The processes and methodology outlined in this book will help you develop internal corporate strategic analysis as it relates to both tactical and strategic alliances. The process of developing strategy involves, first, the synthesis of information; second, development of a vision; third, a decision on the direction for the organization as described in short-, medium-, and long-term strategies; and fourth, the selection of both internal and external options so that implementation in the form of tactics and operations can take place.

Thus, strategy development requires us to ask the question "Where is the company going, now and later?" Once we know the answer, we'll ask another question, "How are we going to get there?" The final question is "Are we implementing our vision appropriately? If not, how do we improve what we are doing?"

Unfortunately, many organizations do not have a clear vision of their long-term direction. They are propelled by short-term tactical or operational needs. Such companies are prone to enter alliances simply because a potential partner approaches them with a proposal. Few are the managers who can exercise the discipline to resist moving into an alliance until they have clarified and decided on the strategic vision for the organization.

One captain of industry in the United States told me recently that his company's strategic opportunities were as yet not clearly defined, although they had many tempting possibilities. Consequently, he refused to enter into any alliance until the fifteen-year strategy was developed. He is the exception.

Another common problem that I have heard discussed by many senior executives is that strategy is well described for the organization in their strategic plan and internal discussions, but when an exciting partner appears, strategy tends to be given short shrift, or is manipulated to fit the partner, rather than the partner's being analyzed for strategic fit with the company. The danger in this will become apparent in Chapters 4 and 5, where we discuss strategic fit and candidate evaluation.

It is not uncommon for an organization to be confused as to whether an alliance is strategic or tactical. Alliances, like companies, are living organisms. Changes in the market or organizational priorities may cause an alliance that was tactical to evolve into one with greater strategic significance, or vice versa. Ultimately, each business defines for itself what activities it considers to be strategic.

The definition of an alliance as strategic or not may greatly influence the role of corporate headquarters in negotiating and monitoring the ongoing alliance activities, especially in larger organizations. A corporate officer, such as the vice president of business development or the officer in charge of strategic alliance development, may not become involved in alliances that are merely tactical. Those activities may be left to the division-level operating managers, who have profit-and-loss responsibility for the alliance. Since tension between corporate headquarters and divisional managers is not uncommon, the distinction between tactical and strategic can be helpful in demarcating areas of responsibility. However, it is important to recognize when an alliance is being *called* strategic, but because of the characteristics of the company and its way of doing business, the alliance is in reality just tactical. Alliance expectations should be aligned accordingly.

There is another important reason why your company should understand the distinction between strategic and tactical: to discover whether there is congruence in the ways you and your potential partner regard the alliance. Is it tactical for them, but strategic for you? If so, you can anticipate a significant difference in the resources each partner will commit to the project, which will have a sizable impact on the alliance's ultimate success or longevity. It is critical to have this information *before* you enter the alliance.

"Mutual Benefit"

Mutuality is the moving target of alliances. It is not a stable element, but rather flows positively or negatively from one partner to the other throughout the life cycle of the relationship. However, keeping one's eye on this target is an essential success factor. The partner who feels that benefits are no longer mutual will most likely be the partner that will consider the relationship to have failed. At times, a benefit that was there at the beginning of the relationship may, as a result of market, industry, or partner changes, no longer be present. Even worse, the benefit may turn into a negative. The concept "mutual benefit" presumes that the relationship is win/win. If the benefit is one-sided at the inception of the relationship, it will be short-lived.

One kind of alliance that is unique because of the inequality of the partners' power is the supplier-purchaser relationship. A problem that commonly occurs is that the purchaser of the product or service speaks the words of alliance but really wants no more than a low-cost, quality supplier, while the supplier prefers to see itself as a full alliance partner, gaining input and knowledge enabling it to develop its products and services, not only at a lower cost but, more important, in a proprietary and collaborative fashion. How disappointed many suppliers have become when their executives realized that what was called an alliance was no more than a purchasing mechanism.

True Alliance or Pricing Squeeze Play?

An oil company that operates worldwide developed a relationship with a supplier of software in the reservoir-management arena. The smaller company was pushing hard for a closer relationship in order to understand more fully the operational needs of the oil company, which would enable new updated versions of the software to be more specific to the oil company's needs. But the oil company, desiring mainly to reduce costs rather than to increase the intimacy of the relationship and have a free exchange of information, wanted to restrict the information access of their supplier. Although the relationship was called a strategic alliance, in fact the oil company considered it mainly a purchasing relationship without any true potential for joint product development.

The reverse scenario also occurs in supplier-purchaser relationships: The supplier is the one mouthing words of mutuality and alliance benefits, whereas their real goal is simply to sell more products to that customer, and not to work with the customer as a partner to jointly develop products for sale elsewhere in the same industry with proprietary and monetary benefits flowing to both companies.

The benefits in both of these instances will come to be viewed as one-sided, and the interests of the partners will over time become incompatible.

Supplier Management in the Automotive Industry

The automotive industry has reached new highs of effective cost control through supplier management. The creation of a tier system for suppliers—large first-tier suppliers subcontract with second-tier companies to provide products and services to the automotive manufacturers—has meant that many supplier companies are struggling to survive in this industry.

"They are slowly and inexorably putting us out of business," says one automotive supplier. He is extremely concerned that his company has mainly expertise but little technology to contribute to the major automotive manufacturer they supply. "Within three years, they will know everything we do about this area." His strategic plan includes a series of strategic alliances in the form of acquisitions in order to reinvent his company. The acquisitions will take him into new industries where he can ease his way out of automotive activity and become a diversified supplier of a variety of services.

How to Turn Adversaries into Partners

An oil industry executive involved in creating a system of supplier management for his company is equally concerned, but for different reasons. "If we don't bring down the costs of production in every area of our business, we won't be here five years from now," he says. "The yield from the reserves in some of our fields will be just too expensive to obtain."

The company decided to replace many smaller companies in a variety of geographic regions with large suppliers with a worldwide presence. However, the executive is encountering hostility within his own organization and resistance to the reduction of the number of suppliers. He has the unenviable task of convincing the members of his organization that this strategy is the right one. Many of the company's subsidiaries and field operators want to use suppliers with whom they have long been familiar and in whom they have developed confidence over time in local areas, rather than to receive an edict from corporate headquarters regarding a specific supplier that must be used.

In addition to managing this internal conflict and dissent, the executive also has to deal with unhappy suppliers. "We are pressuring all our suppliers to work with us on cost and quality. We want to work with them on new products and ways of doing the same tasks differently. But cost and improved performance is what really drives the whole process. No matter how you look at it, mutuality is a requirement for process improvement, but we are in an inherently adversarial relationship."

Though supplier-purchaser alliances use many of the same processes, diagnostics, and methodologies as other strategic alliances, they are very different in a number of areas: They are characterized by the inequality of bargaining positions and by the pressure on cost and quality on the one hand and on increased unit sales on the other. Equally important, because of unequal bargaining power supplier-purchaser alliances often include adversarial, nontrusting relationships, and in that respect and others, I will distinguish them where appropriate throughout this book.

"Compatible or Complementary"

This factor addresses the issue of strategic fit. The question to be asked is "Does the partner organization have characteristics with which you can work, live, learn, and grow?" A competent strategic fit analysis includes considering carefully your internal corporate and managerial personalities and strategy, your options, the relative importance of the criteria for partner selection, and a myriad of other factors. Once you apply the diagnostic and process tools, you will be able to answer the question of compatibility or complementarity with some degree of confidence.

"Business Interests or Goals"

The final concept in the deceptively simple definition of alliances is the business interests or goals of the parties. All too often, organizations have not clearly defined "success," or even "benefit." Their goals may be stated in the negotiation process, but in the implementation of the project, specific aims, milestones, success criteria, and well-defined expectations are neglected. As management and industry changes occur and champions of the project come and go, the initial goals and definitions of success become diluted and confused, and few managers involved in the alliance want to undertake the often unhappy, sometimes career-defining task of examining whether the alliance is still valid or viable.

Each element of our definition of "alliance" is an essential aspect of successful relationships. These elements will be discussed in greater detail as we proceed through the process steps of creating and managing alliances.

Pyramid Analysis: Philosophy Versus Function and Structure of Alliances

One mistake commonly made is to answer the question "What is an alliance?" not from a philosophical perspective but with a functional and structural description, such as "a licensing agreement." Focusing on function and structure misses the point of strategy. Strategy is interrelated with a business's philosophy, vision, hope, and plans for the future. Function and structure follow after the vision is created. The choice of structure (e.g., the legal form of the alliance) must implement the vision appropriately. This means that structures will sometimes be strategic, and other times not. For example, some licensing agreements are strategic, others are not, depending on the vision and goals of the partners.

Our definition of an alliance describes the *philosophy* behind alliances. Choices of structure will follow as a consequence of philosophical decisions or changes in the strategic importance, nature, and increasing or diminishing mutual benefits in the alliance.

Since specific legal structures are not always strategic (e.g., all distribution agreements are not necessarily strategic alliances), they need to be examined for philosophical and strategic integrity. Do the partners have compatible goals? Are the parties deriving mutual benefits? Are the success criteria and goal definitions strategic to the organization? These philosophical issues are explored in depth in Chapters 4 and 5.

Structure is best illustrated by the Pyramid of Alliances, seen in Figure 1-1. The pyramid distinguishes different alliance structures on the basis of three variables: risk, use of human resources, and cost.

A brief explanation of the various kinds of alliances mentioned in the Pyramid of Alliances follows.

Takeover/Merger: The complete acquisition of one company by another. The acquired company often considers this a "merger," while the acquiring company considers it a "takeover."

Joint venture: Two companies cooperate in the creation of a new, separate business entity in order to reach mutually compatible goals.

Equity investment: The purchase of a part of one company's equity by another company for cash, stock, or other consideration.

Research and development partnership: Two companies join in a research project for the development of new technology and/or products for mutual benefit.

Technology transfer: One company transfers knowledge of its technology and the right to exploit it to another company for cash payment or other value.

Original equipment manufacturer (OEM): One company manufactures products to be marketed and sold by another. (This practice is especially prevalent in the computer industry.)

Licensing: One company agrees to provide its know-how to another company for the payment of a consideration, usu-

Figure 1-1: The Pyramid of Alliances

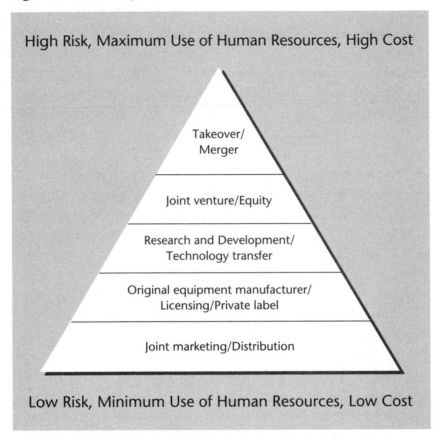

High Risk, Maximum Use of Human Resources, High Cost

Takeover/
Merger

Joint venture/Equity

Research and Development/
Technology transfer

Original equipment manufacturer/
Licensing/Private label

Joint marketing/Distribution

Low Risk, Minimum Use of Human Resources, Low Cost

ally an up-front fee plus royalties (a percentage of sales revenues) for a defined period of time. The agreement can be limited to specific technologies, geographic regions, and/or applications.

Private label: One company manufactures a product for sale under another company's label. (This term is roughly synonymous with "original equipment manufacturer," but is used in most consumer products industries other than computers.)

Joint Marketing and/or Distribution: One company joins with another company in order to market and/or distribute the products of both companies or one company only.

At the inception of the alliance the intent of both parties must be clearly established. For example, the joint marketing or distribution alliance is the lowest-level alliance on the pyramid, because the costs, use of human resources, and risks involved are usually less than those in any other alliance types. But it needn't end there. Many organizations will enter a distribution alliance with the intention of migrating up the pyramid into a more intense kind of relationship, for example, a joint research and development alliance, a joint venture, or a takeover. Such eventualities should be thoroughly aired in the planning stage. In later chapters, you'll see a number of cases where alliance partners were at different levels of expectation on the Pyramid of Alliances and the alliances failed because of that fact.

Distribution Deal: Prelude to a Takeover?

Some alliances that start at the lower level of the Pyramid of Alliances and migrate upward may end up with the sale of one company to another.

The CEO of a small medical diagnostic company had been looking for a distribution partner for some time. The firm was just beginning to generate revenues and needed a partner with credibility in the medical products industry. A distribution agreement was offered by a large medical products company. It seemed generous, but the CEO of the small company was suspicious. "I know that what we are really looking at is the ultimate sale of our technology," he said. "They want to distribute the product, get to understand it well, and then later they will probably offer to buy our company. When that happens, we will have no leverage, since we will be so dependent on them for market access."

The CEO was right. And with this insight, the smaller company realized that the true negotiation was not about the price of the product or any issues regarding its distribution, but rather about the present valuation of their company prior to the planned alliance and its projected value as revenues increased as a result of the relationship.

The smaller company asked: Four or five years after the alliance is in place, what will we have to sell? The larger alliance partner will own most of our value, and the purchase price for our company will be lower than before the alliance existed. On the other hand, the larger company countered, the revenues of the smaller company will have been increased through the distribution efforts of the larger company. Thus, as an acquisition candidate, they would have a higher overall valuation. In effect, the larger company would be paying for a benefit it had helped create.

Fortunately, these differing views of the future were discussed prior to the companies' entering into the distribution alliance. A pyramid analysis helped explain the smaller company's concern that the distribution arrangement would ultimately end up in a sale of either the technology or the company. In this way, the potential long-term risks and opportunities were made part of the alliance negotiation.

The solution for this alliance lay in carefully defining the markets where the products were to be distributed. The distributor was permitted to sell the products only in an agreed-upon market area, and valuation was negotiated with that in mind. The small company's other activities were exempt from the agreement. Seven years later, the larger company agreed to license the technology for that specific market and to manufacture the products themselves. The smaller company was pleased to agree to that, since its focus had meanwhile moved from the medical into the industrial marketplace, where it was growing aggressively.

Pyramid analysis is not only functional and structural. The analysis of the philosophy of partner risk, cost, and commitment of human resources by all partners will raise issues as to differences in expectations. I recommend that the Pyramid of Alliances be put on the table at the beginning of the planning process and that it stay there throughout future discussions. When problems occur, the pyramid can be used as one of the diagnostic tools to track the changes in partner expectations.

There are various names for alliances—alliances, partnerships, relationships—and they will be used interchangeably throughout this book. You will encounter the structural designations for the various types of alliances on the pyramid—distribution, marketing, licensing, research and development, OEM, private label, joint venture, equity investment, mergers, and acquisitions—repeatedly: All are alliances, and all require planning and management. My goal in this book is to improve your skills in doing exactly that.

Alliance fever is sweeping industries of all kinds and sizes. A number of recent surveys have noted this phenomenon, and some of the most significant ones are described below.

The Coopers & Lybrand Survey

The accountancy firm of Coopers & Lybrand, in their 1993 review of fast-growth firms, stated that of the five hundred firms they surveyed, over 55 percent had one or more alliances in place. The percentages of companies reporting various types of strategic alliances were as follows:[2]

Joint marketing or promotional alliance—64%
Joint selling or distribution alliance—52%

Technology license—35%

Design collaboration—34%

Research and development contracts—28%

Production alliances—28%

Other types of "outsourcing"—23%

Clearly, the alliances that are lower on the Pyramid of Alliances are more popular, since they are less risky and require a lower commitment of human resources and capital investment. Note that a low position on the pyramid doesn't necessarily mean that the strategic importance of the alliance is less compelling for the partner companies. "Outsourcing" refers to those activities that are not core competencies and can be done by other companies.

Another reason for the high number of distribution, selling, marketing, and promotional alliances may lie with the partnering company's position in its life cycle. Generally, companies in the early stages of growth are aggressively seeking these kinds of alliances, both domestic and international, to accelerate their growth. Companies in later stages of development might pursue equity partners and acquisitions, joint ventures, licensing of technology, joint R&D, and other measures to move the organization forward or possibly find the magic formula to stay in a fast-growth mode. (In Chapter 2 we will deal in detail with the life-cycle stages of organizations.)

The Caltex Venture

An example of a joint venture by two organizations of similar size and stage of development that has worked extremely well is the Caltex organization. Formed in 1936, it is owned in equal shares by Chevron and Texaco. The alliance was intentionally structured to take advantage of Texaco's extensive marketing resources in the Middle East, Asia, parts of Africa, and Europe, as well as Chevron's large Saudi Arabian reserves and oil resources. The relationship is culturally compatible, with similarities in corporate and managerial cultures—"Once an oilman, always an oilman"—and communication and trust are well developed and managed.

The written contract between Texaco and Chevron is surprisingly simple and leaves many of the details of the relationship to the discretion of the partners. As an executive of one of the partners told me recently, "The amazing part about this relationship was the good faith that was presumed to exist on both sides. Although the alliance became its own organization, separate from the two founding companies, the tremendous goodwill between the parties that came from the fact that they understood each other seemed to propel the concept forward until it could take on a life of its own."

Not all partnerships between organizations in the same stage of the life cycle are successful. But when the corporate and individual managerial personalities are similar and they speak the same language when discussing issues of return on investment (ROI) methods of decision making, and industry knowledge, it does make the base level of mutual understanding that much higher.

One company in the media industry only felt really comfortable with companies that had reached a size that they defined as "material"—over $300 million in annual revenues—and so cut out a series of fast-growth potential partners, emerging companies with exactly the kinds of market knowledge that they were searching for. Though this preference led to some missed opportunities, it was better for them to recognize their corporate preference early in the alliance planning process rather than later, at the negotiating table.

The Ernst & Young Survey

The consultancy firm Ernst & Young reported in 1993 the results of a survey of CEOs from three hundred North American electronics firms from industry segments including computers and peripherals, software, semiconductors and components, aerospace and defense electronics, communications, industrial electronics, and medical and other electronics.[3] Of the companies,

- 65% reported less than $25 million in revenues
- 57% were privately held
- 27% were publicly traded
- 16% were subsidiaries of larger parents

The survey contained a question regarding the companies' activities in domestic and international alliances. The replies established that the industry group was clearly involved in alliances both domestic and worldwide. Of the three hundred firms surveyed,

- 12% were active globally with no alliances
- 27% were domestic with no alliances
- 27% had major domestic alliances
- 32% had multiple locations for major alliances

One observation in the report was that the surveyed companies with under $25 million in annual revenue expected a 200 percent increase in revenue in the next three years, including a 51 percent increase in international sales. The survey found that companies are relying upon alliances as the prime method of implementing global business strategies. The reasons given were access to new markets, enhancement of marketing/sales distribution, access to new technology, improved product development, and defense of market share.

Reasons for Entering into Alliances Given by Non-U.S. Companies

U.S. companies are generally willing to provide straightforward information to surveys. Since the Ernst & Young report is of a survey of U.S. companies, one can assume that the reasons given for alliances are relatively valid and expressed openly. This is not necessarily the case in other cultures, where the reasons given for alliances may represent only a small portion of the real motivation. The survey process may be rejected by these non-U.S. executives as intrusive. If information is given, it may be what is felt to be expected rather than the real data.

Consequently, one must regard another survey, of U.S. and Japanese CEOs, conducted by the consultancy Booz Allen, *The Wall Street Journal,* and the Japanese newspaper *Nihon Keizai Shimbun,* in its cultural context. According to this survey, 74 percent of Japanese CEOs think alliances are effective, and 4 percent think they are dangerous. Although U.S. companies and executives are now open to alliances as never before, as evidenced by both the Coopers & Lybrand and Ernst & Young reports, the Booz Allen et al. survey reported that only 17 percent of U.S. executives considered alliances to be effective, and that fully 31 percent considered them to be dangerous.

Could this relative lack of enthusiasm for alliances have something to do with the fact that the Japanese respondents may have culturally adjusted their answers to what the group expectation is, namely, that alliances are effective? Or is it that we in the United States often would rather talk and teach than learn—and may consequently feel we have given more to an alliance than we have gained from it—while the Japanese would rather listen and learn than teach, gaining knowledge regardless of the nature of ultimate success of the alliance.

In Asia, alliances are a way of life, because proximities of cultures require cross-border relationships. The Lared Group's experience in Europe has shown us that European firms are also involved in numerous alliances large and small. Many are driven by the smallness and proximity of countries and by the interrelationships of communities. Generally, alliances in Europe are seen as a natural and appropriate way of doing business, since companies' "local" market of more than 320 million consumers in Western and Central Europe, now expanding even more to encompass the former Soviet Union, is diverse and international in outlook.

Our clients' activities in Asia are consistent with the European experience: In both settings, many companies choose the market entry approach by means of cross-border alliances.

U.S. companies like the ones surveyed in the Ernst & Young report were once able to build sizable businesses solely in the North American market. Of course, all that has changed. Trade pacts such as GATT, regional treaties such as NAFTA, and regional trade associations such as the EC (European Common Market), CARICOM (a trade pact among Caribbean countries), MERCOSUR (a trade pact among countries in Latin America), and others have changed the world into regional trade areas and have made the U.S. market a competitive hotbed for companies worldwide.

The alliances surveys note some of the important trends in the macro environment that affect what kinds of alliances are appropriate and what kinds will be countercyclical for the near future. Chapter 2 begins our exploration of the kinds of alliances that managers are managing today and can expect to be managing tomorrow.

2.
The Mindshift
Method of
Personality
Diagnostics

In this chapter we explain the Mindshift method of personality diagnostics,★ which will enable you to understand and diagnose the life-cycle stage and personality characteristics of your organization. You'll also learn about the various managerial personality types, each of which fits into specific types of organizations with greater or lesser success. Finally, you'll learn to apply these diagnostic tools to other organizations, individual managers, and the projects on which you or they are working.

Humans have a life cycle—birth, youth, adulthood, midlife, old age, and death—and so do organizations. The stages of the organizational life cycle are characterized by personality changes. If you can diagnose where an organization is in its life cycle, you can predict how it will generally behave.

The organizational life cycle adds an important element to the challenge of managing alliances. Communication can be especially

★ Mindshift is a service mark of Larraine Segil.

complicated between organizations that are in different stages of their life cycles. Mature organizations may have difficulty in understanding what drives a small and entrepreneurial company, and vice versa. Only with an objective, insightful understanding of where our organizations are in their evolutions can we choose appropriate partners and work with them effectively.

Of course, the human life cycle and the organizational life cycle are not perfectly analogous. One difference is that humans cannot restart the cycle from birth to death. Organizations, on the other hand, may survive a "midlife crisis," rejuvenate themselves, and begin the life cycle again as if they were new companies. Though many organizations fail to do this—after a period of growth and success, they stop expanding, fade, and decline—some companies receive the corporate equivalent of an organ transplant and regain much of their youthful quality. This rejuvenation process can also be "managed."

The Mindshift system was developed from observation of over six hundred companies and thousands of executives who have participated in Lared Group programs on strategic alliance process and methodology. Executives from 235 companies applied the system to their own organizations and participated in a follow-up survey.[1] A couple of key points evolved from the survey.* More than half of the participants felt that the personality issues in an alliance became more important over time. Seventy-three percent felt that corporate personality was a frequent contributing factor when alliances failed. Finally, and most important, when alliances failed, *incompatible personality characteristics were found to be a more crucial factor in the failure than any weakness in the business rationale.* Personality diagnostics is the rational application of all the diagnostic tools for identifying personality characteristics presented in this chapter.

* See Appendix D for more information on this survey.

How This Chapter Is Organized

Each section discusses an aspect of the Mindshift method.

The first section describes the five stages in the corporate life cycle.

The second section explains the corporate personality types that operate most comfortably in each stage of the cycle.

The third section identifies individual managerial personality types.

The fourth section discusses strategic alliance types most suitable for use in each stage of the corporate life cycle.

The fifth section explains the exercise managers go through to gauge the importance of the project, a crucial feature of the underlying business rationale for the strategic alliance. From this exercise, the "project personality" emerges. There are three possible types.

The analytical tools in all five sections will give you a better understanding of the critical success and failure factors that affect your ability to enter into and manage successful strategic alliances.

The Corporate Life Cycle

Figure 2-1 is a graphic representation of the corporate life cycle, in which Time and Revenues are the two dimensions.

Stage 1 in the life cycle is the *Start-up*—that of a new and small company, or a new joint venture between two large organizations. One characteristic of a Start-up is that revenues are very small or nonexistent.

Stage 2 is the *Hockeystick* phase. Here the organization sees a rapid growth in revenues, hence the hockeystick image, which refers to the shape of the curve described by the revenue line on the graph in this phase.

Figure 2-1 Diagnostic: The Corporate Life Cycle

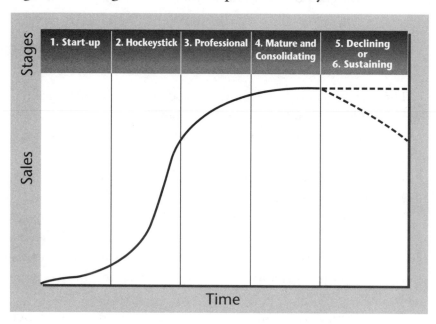

© Copyright 1992, Larraine Segil

Stage 3 is the *Professional* phase. As the company matures, the very rapid growth of its early years generally slows down. Growth in revenues continues, but not at the same rate as during the Hockeystick phase.

Stage 4 is the *Mature and Consolidating* phase. Here revenues gradually level off, as the company completes its penetration of available markets and, in many cases, competition begins to make inroads into the company's territories.

Stages 5 and 6 are alternate directions that a Mature and Consolidating organization can take.

Stage 5, the *Declining* phase, awaits organizations unwilling to change to adapt to new market conditions, the emergence of strong competitors, technological innovations, and other new challenges. Unless an organ transplant is undertaken, a Declining company usually dies, through either bankruptcy or takeover by a stronger firm.

Stage 6 is the *Sustaining* phase, often heralded by the arrival of a visionary manager with a strategy for slowing or reversing the aging process. A truly gifted leader may even be able to launch the firm on a whole new growth cycle, redirecting it into a second Hockeystick phase of rapid growth and expansion.

All the stages are transitory; every company will move into and through each of these stages over time. Naturally, the scheme described here is not an absolute. The changes may occur at very different rates in different companies, and it may not always be clear which stage a company is in. In particular, larger organizations don't always fall entirely into one life-cycle stage or another. Different divisions or business units may be in different stages from each other as well as from the parent company taken as a whole. Consequently, when determining what stage of the life cycle an organization is in, some executives find it more useful to look at each unit of the organization separately. Life-cycle differences among a company's divisions go a long way toward explaining some of the internal issues of communication and style that exist within the organization. The best way to use this approach to analyze an organization or division is to look at a preponderance of factors in each stage, and to make a diagnosis on that basis.

The life-cycle stage of an organization or its divisions is something that most executives can evaluate. Since it is based on revenues over time, it can be represented on a graph or calculated quantitatively. Although many managers will have an intuitive sense of the stage of their division, getting an overview will require a more analytical approach. Categorizing the whole organization as well as the life-cycle stages of different divisions—for both your organization and that of your potential partner—is the first step in clarifying the partners' cultural and stylistic differences and developing a strategy to manage them.

Corporate Personality Types

An organization's stage in the cycle is often manifested not only by the revenue curve but also by certain corporate personality characteristics. Figure 2-2 shows corporate personality characteristics generally associated with the different corporate life-cycle stages.

The reasons for analyzing your corporation's personality type are, first, to recognize the culture and characteristics of the organization within which you operate; then, to understand your com-

Figure 2-2 Diagnostic: Corporate Personality Characteristics

Stage 1. Start-up	**Stage 2. Hockeystick**
Insecure	Confident
Proactive	Quick to react
Emerging	Aggressive
Focus on single goal	Multi-focused
Risk-intense	Lacking management depth
Founder-driven	"Sales come first" philosophy
Noncontinuous delegation	Command and control
	philosophy
Stage 3. Professional	**Stage 4. Mature and Consolidating**
Systematic	Complacent
Planning/Predictive	Protective
Emphasis on marketing,	Risk-averse
not just sales	Rigid administrative structures
Cautious	Form valued over substance
Conflict-resolving	Profit-driven (to reduce costs)
New hires/old fires	Middle management
Consensus-building	proliferates
Stage 5. Declining	**Stage 6. Sustaining**
Overplanning/Budget-driven	Entrepreneurship planned
Ritualistic—form valued	Controlled
over substance	Structurally systematic
Hierarchical	Aggressive
Nonactive (less is more)	Flexibility sufficient to be
Change makers seen as	proactive
problem creators	

© Larraine Segil, 1992

patibility with that organization; and, finally, to use that information to better understand the opportunities and risks of both your organization and yourself as a manager. Do the same for a potential alliance partner, and you will dramatically increase the potential for a well-managed alliance. An alliance's success or failure often depends squarely upon the compatibility of corporate, managerial, and project personalities of its partners.

Stage 1: Start-up

An organization in the Start-up stage will generally be a very exciting place to work, but also an insecure one. Management may have real problems in delegating anything that is even slightly important. Start-up companies have decisive, proactive managers, but these people are often poor at delegation. The Start-up manager often has a such a clear vision of how something should be done that she would rather do it herself than allow someone else to learn by trial and error, as good delegators do.

Time is short and there is a constant sense of urgency in Start-up companies. Yesterday is almost too late. Seven days a week of commitment is needed to create something from nothing, and the drive of the classic Start-up manager is remarkably focused and intense. Thus, by definition, if a Start-up enters into a strategic alliance, the alliance will tend to be all-consuming of management's time and energy, which does not leave much left over for running the actual business. As a result, management by crisis may become the norm. On the other hand, if a company at a later stage of the life cycle has a business problem that needs a new look, a fresh approach, or an unconventional solution, the Start-up company may well be the place to find such input.

Any organization considering an alliance with a Start-up company must ask itself: Do we have the management skills, the cultural understanding, and the communication techniques to work with and satisfy a partner such as this? If not, the alliance is likely to be short-lived. Start-up companies generally have short fuses—and empty pockets. They cannot wait around for Mature and Consolidating or (heaven forbid) Declining organizations to go through thirteen committees to make a decision affecting their business.

Stage 2: Hockeystick

The Hockeystick company seems to be doing everything right. The uncertainties and cash shortages of the Start-up phase are in the past, and the company's revenues are soaring. That fact may make executives at the Hockeystick company arrogant, quick to react, and aggressive. They prefer clear "command and control" management structures rather than flat, team-based approaches, which have processes and systems integrated into their management structures. They also need to control their company's activities as tightly as possible to keep growth from spinning out of control, yet it's likely that the company still has few information and management systems in place. The environment of the Hockeystick company is obviously a challenging one.

It's tough to criticize success, yet regardless of the success of the Hockeystick firm, when they join forces with a Mature and Consolidating or Declining company, conflicts generally ensue. A Mature and Consolidating partner will need the process and systems overlay that are typical of later-stage companies in order to feel comfortable, and that will meet with great resistance from the Hockeystick company, which is accustomed to and will generally prefer the traditional "command and control" model of management power.

Hockeystick companies tend to be governed by the philosophy "Sales come first." Anyone who contributes directly to increased revenues is considered important, and those who don't are not— which may well be what got them successfully over the Start-up hump in the first place. Management staff are often scorned at the Hockeystick firm as unnecessary window-dressing, and so these companies also tend to suffer from a lack of management depth.

Unfortunately, Hockeystick management may become ineffective when the organization grows too large to be driven solely by sales. In an acquisition by or alliance with an organization where revenues are not growing, or are even declining, conflict will inevitably occur, especially if managers from the declining firm try to impose systems, controls, and organizational structures.

"Something's Got to Give"

After the acquisition of a Hockeystick firm by a Declining company in the pharmaceutical diagnostics field, the CEO of the acquired firm, a founder-manager, was still running the company using the military "command and control" approach. Simultaneously, however, professional managers from the headquarters of the acquiring company were working to systematize the organization, flattening out the hierarchy of control and introducing self-directed work teams.

As these two forces moved toward the inevitable showdown, the director of marketing of the acquired company observed to a visitor, "We are heading for a major cultural clash. If our CEO continues to approach the company as if it were his to control, he will not last out the year. He will leave—and why not? He's made a fortune from the acquisition, so the only reason for him to stay is if he is having a good time. And the way things are going, there is a confrontation due almost every time there's a visit from HQ.

"We'll miss him, but, frankly, I'll be rather pleased if things come to a head. The new hires"—post-acquisition recruits, including the director of marketing himself—"are used to professionally managed companies, while the older gang come from the Hockeystick mode. Something has to give, and it won't be the new guys. They paid top dollar to buy the company."

He was right. Four months later the CEO resigned.

The move from Hockeystick to Professional need not involve an ouster at the top. Dell Computers is an example of a company that has transitioned from Start-up through Hockeystick to Professional, while CEO Michael Dell has grown with the company.

Stage 3: Professional

In some ways, the Professional company is the finest with which to develop a strategic alliance. It is a safe and secure place to work—less exhilarating than the Start-up or Hockeystick, but also less volatile. There are usually management and information systems in place, and the growth of revenues is still impressive enough to infuse the organization with a sense of excitement and anticipation. The organization is preparing itself for its longevity and a sprightly and productive middle life.

Founder management may still be involved, and in rare cases the founder may even grow into a professional manager, surrounded by a team of seasoned advisers and implementers. But usually there will be terminations of certain executives carried over from the Hockeystick stage. Sometimes founder management itself has to leave—either because the company is so different that the founder does not feel comfortable there anymore, or because the newly developed professional systems require activities for which he has no skills or respect, such as long-term planning.

The sights of the Professional-phase organization may be focused on other industry players as acquisition targets, and some attempts at diversification may be made into other industry sectors. Planning is a valued process and real marketing skills are added to the company. Compared to the Start-up, management in the Professional company is cautious and good at delegating responsibility, resolving conflict rather than causing it. Consensus building rather than confrontation is one of the characteristics of decision making at a company in the Professional stage of its life cycle.

Stage 4: Mature and Consolidating

Mature and Consolidating companies are often complacent and risk-averse, but they can be effective partners if this tendency to develop rigid administrative structures is recognized and countered. In the technology field, this characteristic can translate into the "Not Invented Here" (NIH) problem: Any technology or expertise developed outside the company is disparaged and dismissed. NIH behavior often starts in this stage of the corporate life cycle and worsens in the next.

Mature companies are heavily administrative, a characteristic that can slow down decision-making and implementation time. This can irritate and undermine a relationship with a Start-up, Hockeystick, or even a Professional company. One rejuvenation technique used by some Mature companies—in particular a defense-industry company that was commercializing some of its technology—is to create a team of managers with fast-track decision-making authority to forge an alliance with a Stage 1, 2, or 3 company.

Middle management proliferates in Mature companies, which also can add to the time involved in creating or justifying and ultimately implementing decisions. Form may become more important in decisions than substance. Even the form in which profits are pursued often changes when a company enters this phase: Whereas companies in earlier stages of development seek revenue growth, Mature firms often turn instead to cost cutting.

Stage 5: Declining

Over time, good employees tend to leave Declining companies. Those who stay and try to effect change are often considered troublemakers and are forced out. What's left are those who have become part of the problem.

Death by Memo

An aerospace company executive who attended my course spent a fair amount of time bemoaning the fact that his organization was deeply into the Declining phase. A few weeks later, I called him with a specific opportunity. A major company in the medical device arena wanted a strategic partner, and it appeared that the aerospace firm might be a suitable fit. It appeared there was a significant business opportunity for both parties.

When I called, however, the executive's secretary told me that he had a policy: No one could have a conversation with him unless they first put in writing the reason they wanted to talk. I explained that I knew him, he'd attended my course. It was no use. The policy was rigid.

Accordingly, I wrote a memo giving the general outline of the alliance opportunity. When I made a follow-up call a few weeks later, the secretary told me that her boss was overwhelmed with paperwork at the moment (not surprisingly) and would not be able to read or respond to the memo for some time. "Well, can you tell him I've called?" I asked. "Oh no," she said, "he'll have to read your memo first. Then he'll decide whether to take your call!"

Needless to say, the business opportunity went elsewhere. The future for this company looks bleak.

Declining companies are the antithesis of Start-up companies. They overplan and are budget-driven. An enormous amount of an executive's time is involved in paperwork and memo writing, activities designed to justify decisions and spread the risk so that he or she cannot be blamed personally for an action. This kind of environment encourages inaction; change makers are seen as problem creators. The movement of the organization toward "ritualistic" behavior—cumbersome procedures as to who should be copied on memos, excessive meetings, protocol about who calls meetings—pushes the concept of form over substance to a new high. Although there may be talk of "self-directed work teams" and "empowerment," the real corporate structure involves hierarchical or complex, matrix-based (overlaid, interconnecting) reporting designs that keep most of the employees confused most of the time.

All may not be lost, however. The arrival of a visionary manager may jump-start the organization into Stage 6, Sustaining mode.

Stage 6: Sustaining

If a company has reached Stage 5, Declining, in order to survive the entire organization will ultimately have to be turned inside out, and its thinking mechanisms, problem-solving approaches, reward systems, and other key organizational and cultural features must change dramatically, under the leadership and inspiration of a visionary manager. A first step in this complex process is to make the company a place where new ideas are welcomed, rewarded, and implemented. This will infuse energy into those managers who respond, squeeze out those who resist, and attract a different breed of proactive management—management that anticipates problems and opportunities and implements actions and solutions. Only then can the organization start to break up the structures, rules, and bureaucracy that have slowly been destroying its life.

Organizations engaged in this process of change gradually attain the Sustaining phase. Losing divisions or those that do not fit with the core competencies of the organization are spun out or closed down. In this way, the company regains some level of flexibility, as the visionary leader and his team move the Declining company into Sustaining mode. The changes that have been happening in Kodak since the arrival of George Fisher from Motorola are characteristic of a Sustaining organization where proactive management is infused into the rigidity of the existing structure and aggressive new strategies are implemented. Mr. Fisher's activities as a visionary leader are further explored in Chapter 3.

Individual Managerial Personality Types

Up to this point, you have been analyzing your company and its various divisions and have come up with a rough idea of their corporate life-cycle stages and personalities. But in the back of your mind you may be asking, "Where do I fit into the scheme of things? Am I a useful advocate of change, or perhaps part of the problem? Am I in the right company at the wrong time?" This section will help you start to answer some of these questions. As Figure 2-3 indicates, there are five main managerial personality types.

Type 1: The Adventurer

The first managerial personality type is the *Adventurer,* most often found in Start-up companies.

The Adventurer is the ultimate risk taker, and he combines that quality with an absolute and unshakable belief in his vision. This often reaches the level of an obsession, which is also sometimes unrealistic. His sense of urgency, however, will compel venture capitalists to invest seed capital in his idea, and his drive to realize his dream may convince others to back his hopes and fund his grand designs. Typical examples of the Adventurer are the company founder, or the manager who wants an answer to a problem yesterday.

Adventurer managers are not necessarily company founders. Remember that Start-up companies are not exclusively small, entrepreneurial organizations, a Start-up may be the joint venture of two established, possibly Mature or Declining, organizations, where the Adventurer is the new organ in the organ transplant. Managers found in the joint-venture kind of Start-up are not always transplanted Adventurers, since the large parent organizations may import their existing people to staff the new entity. Even so, those willing to take the risk of being involved in anything different from the protective world in which they already live will have some of the personality characteristics of the Adventurer.

In the early 1980s, many corporations seeking technology breakthroughs both within and outside their own industries, poured millions into captive venture funds—funds that are capital-

Figure 2-3 Diagnostic: Managerial Personality Types

1. Adventurer
Risk taker
Has personal vision
Obsessive
Driven
Sometimes unrealistic
Sense of urgency

2. Warrior
Aggressive
Self-confident
Wins battles (may lose war)
Abrasive
Result-focused
Resistant to process
Omnipresent

3. Hunter
Leader
Good team and consensus
    builder
More formal
Systematic

4. Farmer
Member of old boy network
Formal
Risk-averse
Conforms in behavior

5. Politician
"Cover your rear"
    (CYA) philosophy
Risk-averse
Polite but self-protective
Emphasizes form over substance
    in behavior
Uses paperwork as protection
    against reality
Isolationist
Bureaucratic

6. Visionary
Results-oriented
Assertive
Confident
Inspires hope, empowerment
Team builder
Risk taker
Flexible

© 1992 Larraine Segil

ized by money set aside by a corporation to be invested in high-risk ventures. Large sums were made by some and lost by others. Today's more mature and sophisticated venture-capital community still has vast sums for investment, but it is demanding that the Adventurer managers meet higher and more exacting standards. However, as long as "big win" outcomes can be made—for example, the 1995 initial public offering of Netscape, a Start-up that is fast becoming a Hockeystick—there will continue to be Start-ups created by Adventurers.

The Adventurer manager's wonderful self-confidence should be recognized, but so should his lack of patience with the management process—often expressed as an unwillingness to delegate, monitor, allow for errors, and correct a subordinate's actions—and his unilateral decision-making style. The Adventurer may find it hard to develop realistic expectations for a company's later life-cycle phases. In an alliance with a Mature and Consolidating company, the Adventurer must learn to patiently accept that his counterpart in the partner company may not have ultimate decision-making authority. Such discrepancies of practices and expectations can start to eat away at a relationship unless they are anticipated and planned for.

Type 2: The Warrior

The Hockeystick-stage company generally attracts the *Warrior* manager.

It's very exciting to be around this kind of manager. Some are young, even still in their early twenties, for example, in the computer hardware and software industries. Successful Warriors fly very high. Their profiles appear in *Inc.* magazine, soon to be followed by *Forbes* or *Fortune,* and they are the darlings of Wall Street if their companies are well known to the public. Their every move is a matter of journalistic interest, as they are observed closely for their daring, their triumphs, and their mistakes.

The Warrior manager is one who is a charismatic leader, directing, controlling, inspiring, and motivating those who work for him, most of whom mirror his energy and commitment.

Meanwhile, the wise advisers to the Warrior, often in the background, who mutter about "process" and "professionalism" are often ignored or merely tolerated. That's because when one is riding high with success, it is easier to be aggressive than reflective. And in many cases the Warrior's success continues for a long time. However, it's important that she realize that everything—including businesses—moves in cycles, so that she and her company can be prepared for the inevitable changes time and growth will bring.

Bill Gates of Microsoft, Larry Ellison of Oracle Systems, Steve Jobs, formerly of Apple and Next, George Rathmen of Amgen, Michael Dell of Dell Computer—these are some of the best-known Warrior managers of the past two decades. So far they have all achieved a lasting measure of success. Many Warrior managers are not so fortunate. In some cases, their careers fizzle when the fit between them and their companies stops working, or when the concept on which they based their initial success loses its timeliness. When this happens, the Warrior's aggressive, self-confident, sometimes abrasive approach begins to backfire. They may be ousted from the companies they helped to start, or may go down with the ship when their firms founder in changing markets.

Type 3: The Hunter

The *Hunter* manager is most often found in Professional companies.

Hunters work well with team-based processes. They enjoy building consensus, and will sometimes bring needed structure and formality into a previously chaotic corporate situation, although these circumstances will vary by industry. Hunters demand that organizational results be tracked and measured to enhance accountability, and introduce the mechanisms, such as long-term strategic planning, that are typical of professionally managed companies. These concepts may have been given short shrift by Adventurer managers, who plan mainly in order to satisfy the requirements of their investors, and Warriors, who find it difficult to think in time spans greater than one to three years.

It's not unusual for the Hunter never to have been involved in a Start-up. He may well be an escapee from a Mature and Consolidating company or even one that is moving into Decline. He is comfortable with accountability and controls and is an excellent people person, with his own ego well under control. He is a superb listener and has good skills in managing creative and entrepreneurial people.

When a Hunter joins a growing company, one in the Start-up or Hockeystick phase, he and his team often move slowly into place, one at a time, introducing collaborative skills and team-building empowerment tools that enable the firm to take the best qualities of Stage 2 and formalize the operation into Stage 3. Very often a Hunter is able to work with his Warrior predecessor and refocus him into specific activities of the company for which he is suited, such as marketing, public speaking, and development and articulation of a strategic vision, rather than performing an operating role. If the Warrior's ego cannot be tamed sufficiently so that his skills can be applied for the corporate good, he may have to be "kicked upstairs" into an honorary position or moved out of the company altogether. In some cases, the Warrior may even prefer to leave. Since the company isn't "his" anymore—"not the same place, no freedom, no excitement"—he may already be thinking about his next entrepreneurial venture, planning the next "big kill."

From Warrior to Hunter

A major Professional-stage organization in the field of human immunology research that recently acquired a Hockeystick company and its Warrior manager has, through its Hunter managers, been patiently exposing the abrasive Warrior to its professional methods.

"It's rather painful," one of the firm's senior executives explained recently. "We wanted the guy for his charisma and drive, but he is very resistant to process. In our industry, relationships with the Food and Drug Administration require a systematic approach. Additionally, our credo calls for marketing only the highest-quality products. The company we acquired used to grab market share by sometimes bringing products to the market too soon, but now they're part of us. To maintain our worldwide reputation for high-quality, zero-defect products, we have to slow him down and smarten him up. He's not happy, but he is listening. We expect he'll come around and learn our ways." The education process is continuing, as the Warrior becomes the Hunter.

The Return of the Adventurer

A certain Adventurer manager was extremely successful in using an alliance to transfer aerospace technology into a Start-up company that became a Hockeystick in the transportation industry. However, the next company launched by the same Adventurer-led team of venture capitalists struggled along as one of the living dead for years as everyone involved waited for history to repeat itself. It never did.

Finally, the company hired a professional manager, a Hunter, who redirected the company into a new market area. The venture capitalists and the Hunter called us in to help develop a strategy for growth. We designed a strategy that included a distribution alliance for the company's key product with a partner in the same industry that had both domestic and international sales. The strategic fit was good and the alliance went well, but the market was limited and growth was still modest. The Adventurer continued to be disappointed.

In the end, the Hunter became frustrated with the Adventurer's lack of realism regarding the product's capability and the firm's inability to move past the Start-up into the Hockeystick phase. He saw a better use of his skills elsewhere and left. The brilliant and eccentric Adventurer founder regained his hold over the company. Today, the company continues to struggle along, each new opportunity and market option being infused with Adventurer-type excitement, but without the needed thoroughness that the Hunter could have offered. The hoped-for Hockeystick phase has not yet evolved.

Building Toward a Successful Initial Public Offering (IPO)

A midwestern industrial-device manufacturer recruited a new company president a few years before the company was to go public. He fit all the criteria for a Hunter manager. He was able to accommodate new and creative ideas and could work effectively with technology experts.

Even new ideas that were outside their industry area got a hearing. In one successful instance, a technology application developed within the firm had the potential to transcend the company's industry segment, crossing over into the industrial-safety area. Had the company tried to develop it as an independent manufacturing project, it probably would have sapped the resources of the company. Instead, they developed it as a product idea for license to an industry leader in that area. In choosing the appropriate strategic alliance strategy—licensing the technology rather than manufacturing and distributing the product—this Hunter manager focused the organization on its core business, helping them move toward a public offering and continued success.

Type 4: The Farmer

The Farmer manager is usually found in Mature and Consolidating companies. He is seasoned, one who has the patience needed to sow seeds and wait for them to mature—hence, the Farmer moniker. Sometimes he becomes complacent, and market changes can take him by surprise. In the Mature and Consolidating firm complacency is a sign that corporate sclerosis may be setting in. But there is usually sufficient flexibility left in the organization to allow for some innovation. However, since the Farmer manager is usually a member of the Old Boy Network whose behavior is conforming and formal, he will verify all his decisions carefully with friends and colleagues within the company to be sure that he will not be risking his reputation if the decision fails.

A Farmer managing a successful Mature and Consolidating company often has capital to invest in an alliance with a cash-hungry Hockeystick company, and the partnership can be quite successful. However, the Hockeystick's Warrior manager will have to curb his impatience in dealing with the Farmer, since taking chances is not easy for Farmers, who believe in conservation and protection and are generally risk-averse.

Type 5: The Politician

Sadly, *Politicians* abound in Declining companies. The most regrettable quality of the Politician is her tendency to take a perfectly valid business opportunity and kill it through self-protective activities, delaying tactics, political game playing, and fear of action. When a Start-up company tries to create an alliance with a Declining company, they often find, to their dismay, that their Politician partner effectively "details" them to death, killing the project. The demise of the Declining company itself may follow soon after.

Death by Details

A division of a well-known company involved in artificial intelligence software was approached by a Start-up company seeking a business partner to help them market their innovative neural network technology. The initial reaction was favorable, and further discussions began. The Start-up firm provided enormous amounts of information, often gathered in round-the-clock and weekend hours by their tireless Adventurer manager, working with a small band of devoted software programmers.

The Start-up firm was highly motivated because their own business situation was financially shaky. In fact, as the negotiations progressed, they saw this alliance as the only opportunity left for them; they were at the end of their resources and waiting, gasping, for the promised infusion of capital from their larger partner. "Just a few more items of information and the funding will follow," the Declining company executive promised.

The smaller company now was in a rapid downward spiral; they had no more resources to apply to another potential partnership or even the time to look for one and no immediate funding in sight from their prospective partner. Meanwhile, the demands for information, driven more by bureaucracy than by real technology concerns, continued. Finally, the whole process collapsed, leaving the Adventurer manager furious and frustrated. "I had to let the team go. We couldn't make payroll, and the partnership died in the process of being born. What a foolish waste."

The Declining company itself was taken over and liquidated soon after the collapse of their erstwhile Start-up partner. The brilliant technology developed by the Start-up was licensed to a competitor as part of the dissolution of assets in liquidation. Many other Start-up technologies are even less fortunate; they disappear into the sea of great ideas that never made it.

The Politician manager is totally risk-averse. One former executive of a company in decline gave me the best job description I have heard for the Politician manager: "Her job is to cover her rear—plain and simple. That's all she does. She learns to write memos in such a way that paperwork is a protection against reality."

The Politician manager interacts in varying ways with other types of managers. She is unlikely to survive in a Hockeystick company; the Warrior manager will find her out immediately and show little tolerance for her time-wasting tactics. The Adventurer manager will not understand a word the Politician says as she buries any position she might actually believe in under a layer of pleasantries and chat; the Politician is similarly mystified by and uncomfortable with the Adventurer's directness.

Hunter and Farmer managers will both recognize the Politician and understand her modus operandi. The Hunter is unlikely to want a Politician in his organization; if he is saddled with one, he will isolate her where she can do the least amount of damage. The Farmer is far more likely to tolerate the Politician manager. After all, he is but one step away from that stage himself.

Type 6: The Visionary

What a relief it is to come across a Visionary manager! A strong Visionary manager inspires hope and empowerment through his results-oriented, assertive, and confident demeanor. He generally enters a Declining company with a breath of promise to transform it into a Sustaining one. His challenge is to take a company that is highly structured and formalized with many layers of management and streamline it to make it more flexible.

The Visionary has some of the characteristics of the Adventurer—his inspirational approach and intense drive, for example—but he is more experienced and measured in his style. The Visionary manager has usually been a professional Hunter manager for a substantial period of his life, and is familiar with the Politician types, too; he can spot them a mile off, and will isolate or terminate them in large numbers. Where he differs greatly from the Adventurer and Warrior is in his ability to build teams while still taking risks and bringing about systematic change.

The Visionary manager is usually accompanied by his team—a small group of leaders who may have been with him in former turnarounds or helped him succeed in other past activities. They will help improve the serious morale problems that often exist in the company the Visionary enters.

Stemming Decline Through an Alliance Infusion

The senior vice president of a chemicals company has seen its market changing for the worse and is trying to accelerate itself into a new market area. This manager's responsibility is to find and implement alliances that will sustain the growth of the organization and hopefully help transform a Declining organization into a Sustaining one. The company has $175 million in annual revenues and thirteen hundred employees; the division managed by this senior VP has $38 million in annual revenues and three hundred employees.

The senior VP identified as a potential partner a Start-up firm with twenty employees and $1.5 million in annual revenues. The Start-up manager is clearly an Adventurer with all the good and bad characteristics that implies. In particular, he is resistant to process. But he and his company have product and marketing connections in an industry in which the larger firm has none. The Declining company VP is a Hunter (not a good fit with his own company), with one characteristic of a Politician—he is highly risk-averse.

The early stages of the proposed relationship were troubled, largely owing to communications difficulties between the two managers—not surprising, given their marked differences in personal management style. We recommended that the chemical company VP create an alliance implementation plan that called for fast-track decision making, the development of clear, project performance checkpoints for monitoring partnering activity, and a close liaison relationship with the Adventurer manager. The interpersonal connection should focus on affirming and recognizing the Adventurer's excitement, enthusiasm, and need to move swiftly while honoring the project milestones that had been jointly negotiated. If this is done, the alliance should be able to infuse new energy into the Declining company without hampering the creativity and responsiveness of the Start-up partner.

Company Stage and Managerial Personality

Although organizations in a certain stage of their life cycle will tend to attract managers that fit that stage, mismatches between a manager and the company in which he finds himself are not uncommon. Furthermore, as a company grows and moves from one stage into another, managers that fit before may find difficulty in adjusting later.

A "nonfit" manager will suffer many frustrations, since his value system and rewards will be out of step with those of the larger culture within which he is functioning. A manager in this position has a number of options. He can simply tolerate the mismatch, which normally means operating under a high degree of personal stress and unhappiness. He can move aggressively to bring about change within his unit, group, division, or even the whole company, trying to make the organization more closely match his personal style and his vision for the firm. He may be able to develop a particular project in which his managerial personality is accepted or even rewarded, and in that way preserve a positive place in the corporate infrastructure. Or he may leave the company or change division or group.

In any case, understanding the corporate life cycle and how it relates to managerial personality types can help greatly in the diagnosis of stresses and frustrations and alleviate the need to blame, discourage, criticize, and demoralize those who do not fit neatly into their company's corporate personality. Rather, by recognizing the differences, it is possible to design team or individual approaches that creatively utilize a mismatched manager's specific management strengths.

I do *not* advocate that organizations hire or keep only those who fit the corporate personality. Pablo Picasso said, "To copy oneself is more dangerous than to copy others. It leads to sterility." An organization that can incorporate many different managerial personalities, not just those individuals who feel comfortable in the company's stage of the corporate life cycle and personality, will draw strength from the resulting diversity.

Strategic Alliances in Different Stages of the Corporate Life Cycle

Certain specific kinds of strategic alliances predominate at each stage of the corporate life cycle. Although many kinds of strategic alliances are appropriate at any one of the stages, the organizational issues at different stages mean that some structures are used more commonly than others.

For example, strategic alliances that are commonly seen in Start-up organizations are equity investments, research and development relationships, or collaborative bidding and development joint ventures. Also very common in the Start-up phase are distribution, marketing, and licensing alliances. This is because organizations that have a low level of revenue will need to gain access to the market as well as to grow and generate income. These alliance structures are common ways to achieve those goals.

In the Start-up or Hockeystick stage, companies will often develop international versions of these alliances, once the product or service concept has proved itself in the home market. One exception to this is in biotechnology and defense-related organizations, which often create international licensing arrangements before product launch.

Strategic equity alliances are common in Stages 1 to 3, but acquisitions are more common in Stage 3, the Professional stage. The Professional organization has systems and professional Hunter managers in place and is still growing, at least modestly. Acquisitions are seen as a way to accelerate growth, integrate new market extensions, or add critical market share.

By contrast, companies in the Mature and Consolidating stage will often divest themselves of unwise or unsuccessful acquisitions. By this time, revenues have flattened out and the results promised by the acquisition may not have materialized, owing either to poor postacquisition integration or to changes in the market or industry, so that the added overhead without accompanying increases in

Figure 2-4 Diagnostic: The Corporate Life Cycle and Strategic Alliances

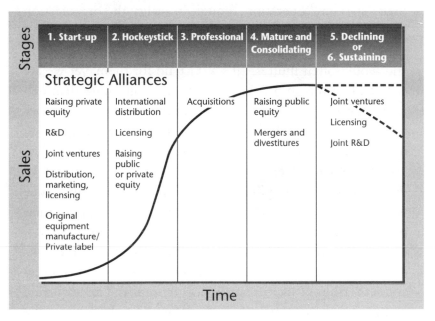

revenues or profits make divestiture more appealing than maintaining the status quo.

Finally, organizations in the fifth stage, Decline, often try to make the transition into Sustaining companies by means of new and invigorating joint ventures in research and development or licensing.

Life-Cycle Stages: Perceived and Genuine

When one company acquires another as a way of entering a new market area or developing a new business expertise, the acquiring company may refer to the newly owned venture as a "start-up," even though it may be a Hockeystick or possibly even a Mature and Consolidating company.

This occurred recently when a computer peripherals company made one such acquisition and kept referring to it as their "start-up" operation, though in reality the organization was in the Hockeystick stage when acquired. The management that were acquired were extremely irritated by the term and would often mutter, "It's a start-up for them, yet we are old hands at this stuff." The dispute involved more than terminology. The acquired firm felt that the value of their experience was discounted by the acquirers. As one manager put it, "If only they would listen to us, they could save themselves mistakes. We'd prefer if they'd get out of the way and let us grow. They are trampling on the very expertise that they wanted from us and that we possess, in order to impose their processes and systems." As a result, the acquisition has not been well integrated into the larger firm. Treating the Hockeystick company like a Start-up has undermined the abilities and leadership of its management. The result? The acquiring company is killing the goose that lays the golden egg—the company they paid for.

The telecommunications industry provides an interesting current example of how alliances take place against the backdrop of the corporate life cycle. Most senior executives from telecommunications companies are looking at an entirely new world as they try to position themselves for the future. The Regional Bell Operating Companies (RBOCs) are generally companies in the Mature and Consolidating stage, which are uncertain as to whether their corporate cultures will lead them to sustain or decline. They need to ally themselves with organizations in other industries that can utilize their market reach, database management, telecommunications traffic control, and switching skills. This is because competitors are arising in their markets with skills and technologies that can access customers who formerly were the captive audience of the traditional telephone company. The wiser of the RBOCs are realizing that they also need to learn the skills of market "pull" as opposed to technology "push"—to become customer-oriented in a variety of market niches in a competitive world where they no longer have a monopoly on the telephone link.

It is not known whether the partners in the myriad RBOC alliances being entered into today have ever addressed the personality and life-cycle issues described here. The jury is still out as to how many such alliances will last beyond the three-to-five-year time span.

A Start-up Emerges from Two Late-Cycle Companies

During the days of the defense build-up in the United States, two large aerospace companies joined together in a joint venture set up specifically to bid on a major federal request for proposals (RFP) for the manufacture of certain weapons systems. The alliance took on many of the characteristics of both companies, one of which was in the Mature and Consolidating phase and the other, in the Declining phase.

Nevertheless, the Start-up personality emerged in several ways. For example, managers had to take individual responsibility for their actions rather than make decisions by committee. Support from corporate staff was nonexistent, and the project required self-starter type managers who were proactive and prepared to take some risk. So even though one would expect the new joint venture to have the personality of the parent companies, the venture was neither Mature nor Declining, but rather a different kind of Start-up.

The Start-up characteristics—proactivity, initiative, and a sense of urgency—caused consternation and surprise in some of those who felt comfortable with the corporate cultures of the venture's "parents." The managers who took part successfully in the new venture were seen by their former colleagues as renegades. Fortunately, the executive who ran the new operation was wise enough to hire and develop people with the drive to bring about change and the ability to face new challenges comfortably.

Project Personality Types

The last factor in this intricate web of relationships that must be taken into account is the Project Personality Type (see Figure 2-5). Even when the compatibility of organizations and managers is high, this factor may doom the alliance to failure all by itself if the organizations assign differing levels of importance to the project. A project that is of fundamental, even survival, importance to one company may be just a sideshow to the other. This will affect the resources—staff, money, time—committed to the project. Every aspect of the alliance is affected by the Project Personality Type, from negotiating the deal points to the choice of managers to run the alliance, and, most important, the follow-up and continuing commitment of the two partners to the project. Analyzing Project Personality Types is, therefore, a two-step process. First, identify which Project Personality Type you think describes your project, then have your potential partner identify the type that they feel best fits their conception of the project. Then, both parties must adjust their expectations and management approach so that both derive the best return from the project, especially if the partners take different views of the Project's Personality Type.

Let's describe the different kinds of alliance projects and their importance to their respective partners.

Project Type 1: Bet the Farm
A Bet the Farm project is of crucial financial and strategic importance to the company that undertakes it. Very often, Start-up companies are involved in this type of project. When a Start-up is

Figure 2-5 Diagnostic: Project Personality Types

1. Bet the Farm projects...
- are integral to future survival of corporation—fit into macro strategy and positioning.
- are well financed.
- have top-management involvement.

2. Market Extending projects...
- are of secondary importance, e.g., U.S. market is major thrust, international market seen as secondary.
- represent part of a medium-term business strategy re implementation—with some macro or long-term elements.
- have some top management involvement at their inception, but it wanes over time unless the alliance becomes Hockeystick.

3. Experimental projects...
- are of limited importance to top management but are vital to segments of organization, e.g., R&D.
- have committed resources limited vis-à-vis time and results.
- don't have well-designed conflict resolution mechanisms.

© 1992 Larraine Segil

engaged in a Bet the Farm project with a larger, more established company, they will often be concerned about the "ant and elephant syndrome," that is, inequality of bargaining position of the two parties. They will fear that the project could be of minimal importance to their partner but critical to them. The communication problems between the partners in this kind of situation can be intense. The fears of the smaller company that they have no other options or may be excluded from other market opportunities as a result of their alliance with a particular partner can generate a level of urgency and tension from the start.

One manager whose small firm was running an annual loss of $20,000 voiced the concern that they had no second chance at partnership; either their current alliance worked, or they were out of business. That is often the meaning of Bet the Farm for smaller companies. Larger companies, however, can also be involved in a Bet the Farm alliance. It can be a venture that represents a directional shift that is pivotal to how they see their future, even though they will not necessarily be out of business if it fails. Such a project will get top management attention, be well financed, and have a longer time frame within which to succeed than projects in the other categories.

Type 2: Market Extending

The Market Extending project is one designed to help expand a company into a market that is secondary to its major market; an example would be where the major market is the United States and the international market is secondary. These kinds of relationships often start to fall apart within three to five years unless they attain Hockeystick-type success. This is because of the relatively minor importance of the project—some resources will be allocated to it, but management will need to be convinced that it is worth funding or supporting in the long term. The only way to do that will be by results and success.

This is particularly true with U.S.-based public companies, whose perspectives are dominated by quarterly issues; they see three to five years as a long time in which to prove the value of a business concept. Some technologies, such as speech recognition, and certain markets, such as the evolution of CD-ROM or superconductors, by their very nature require a much longer time line. So if your partnership has a Market Extending character, it will be important in the planning stages of the relationship to establish both partners' understanding of the meaning of the phrase "long term." Otherwise, waning management attention may doom the project just when it is beginning to show promise.

It is also critical in negotiations not to raise expectations too high. Adventurers and Warriors tend to do this, but the Hunter or Visionary manager can temper projections with her wider and more moderate perspective.

Type 3: Experimental

Experimental projects are generally of limited importance to top management, but could be vital to segments of the organization, such as R&D. Resources will be committed to the project but they will also be limited in terms of time (there will be a time limit on resource availability) and results (concrete results may be expected within a limited time frame). When these kinds of projects fall on troubled times, the conflict resolution mechanisms that might give a longer life to more important projects, for example those that are Bet the Farm, are apt to fail, and the project is likely to be canceled.

The project personality is also relevant to the issue of whether an alliance is strategic or tactical. It is rare that an Experimental alliance will be strategic, whereas Bet the Farm projects by definition are strategic in nature.

Applying the Mindshift Method

The Mindshift method is using the diagnostic tools to analyze your own company and your prospective partner. It is a process that should be facilitated by an objective person with no particular bias toward any personality type or stage of the corporate life cycle. The best approach is as follows:

1. *First, discover the stage of the life cycle that your unit, division, group, or organization is in.* This is done by relating revenues or units of growth to time. In most cases, looking at the fi-

nancials for each company or division will confirm what most of the managers who work in that division or company already know about the organization's place in the corporate life cycle.

2. *Determine the organization's corporate personality.* Look at the personality characteristics listed for each type of company and identify the ones that fit your group, unit, division, or company. They may "belong" to various stages of the life cycle. If so, try to determine which personality type accommodates most of your company's characteristics.

3. *Look at your personal managerial characteristics to see how you fit within the stages of corporate cycles of change.* Again, you may find that a blend of qualities from more than one personality type best describes you. Try to identify for yourself the single managerial type most fully descriptive of you. Then have one or more colleagues evaluate your self-perception—I do this in a group exercise. The result can be a perception by group members that differs quite consistently from your own assessment of your management style and skills, which can lead you to reevaluate the way you manage others. (This evaluation process can also be used to select team members who will be used in alliance planning and implementation.)

4. *Examine the project personality characteristics.* Determine the level of importance to each partner of the existing or proposed alliance.

5. *Use the diagnostic tools to analyze your actual or prospective partner as you have analyzed your own company and managers.*

6. *Finally, develop strategies based on observed personality differences that will allow you and your partner to communicate.* This may mean adjusting or creating new management structures by changing the form of the alliance to realign goals, migrating up or down the Pyramid of Alliances, modifying project priorities, or realistically reformulating the project's expectations, milestones, or expected results. The measures undertaken might be something as simple as respecting the

different urgency levels of managers at the partnering companies by compromising on response times for requests for information.

Although all-purpose strategies cannot be prefabricated, here are examples of some that have worked, to illustrate the kind of thinking that is required:

- Problem: Hockeystick company in alliance with Mature and Consolidating company, where project personality is Bet the Farm for the Hockeystick and Market Extending for the Mature.
- Solution: Create a fast-track decision process that will appeal to Warrior managers by choosing a small group of managers within the Mature company that have Hunter personalities rather than Farmers. The sense of urgency of the Warrior will be satisfied by a more speedy decision cycle than is normal for Mature companies. Then explain the need for proof of concept in order to sustain the project at the Market Extending level and lift it into Hockeystick growth to keep the interest of the Mature company high.

- Problem: A Start-up company in alliance with a Professional company, where the project is Bet the Farm for the Start-up but Experimental for the Professional.
- Solution: Look for Adventurer- or Warrior-type managers within the Professional organization. They will be able to re-assure the Adventurer manager that she and her project will not be ignored while making clear that there is a defined time within which she has to perform or funds will be cut. Avoid overlaying systems or reporting mechanisms until the concept has been proved; visit the company, observe the action or lack thereof, but reduce the amount of paperwork required until the project grows from Experimental to Market Extending. Since the Start-up company has no middle management, the

Adventurer has few if any resources to devote to record keeping, reporting, and meetings.

Developing strategies for using these tools has to be done on an ad hoc basis. No two situations are exactly the same.

Summary

The above characterizations of Corporate Life-Cycle Stage and Corporate Managerial and Project Personality Types have a practical purpose. Understanding them will enable you to

- Clarify internal conflicts and inconsistencies within your own organization
- Predict your company's predisposition to various kinds of alliances
- Discover whether the right managers are spearheading the alliance process
- Analyze how rapidly your partner will respond to changes in the environment
- Understand how decisions will be made
- Recognize what control issues will get in the way
- Realize how insecurity and bureaucracy will affect performance and response times
- Uncover other issues related to differing corporate personalities, cultures, and values

In the chapters that follow, we'll explore ways to ensure that your company has its global strategy and vision in place—a prerequisite to entering any strategic alliance—and has created a sound process for developing, implementing, and evaluating alliances, domestic or international.

3.
Integrating Alliances into Corporate Strategy

Alliance strategy must be integrated into overall corporate strategy, articulated in the strategic plan with a process for implementation. Unfortunately, many managers struggle to balance the often conflicting demands of planning vs. implementing. Consequently, we've developed a short-cut methodology for assisting companies in the strategic planning process. Strategic planning per se will not be covered here. What I will address is a process for arriving at well-implemented alliances that fits within strategic planning.

Planning for Alliances

The entire process of developing and managing an alliance should follow these steps:

1. Development of the strategic plan, domestic or global
2. Development of the alliance plan

3. Partner search and selection
4. Development of the implementation plan
5. Execution of the implementation plan

Developing the Strategic Plan, Domestic or Global

Clearly, alliances are not part of every organization's strategic plan. They are but one of many options of a broad-based strategy. The integration of alliance strategy into the overall strategy of the organization will depend on the extent of your vision of the future for the company.

You can look at strategy in a number of ways. Remember the difference between strategy and tactics. Tactics are developed while you are engaged in operations. Strategy is thought of and planned for in advance of engagement and operations and can then be implemented in the present-, medium-, or long-term future. Tactics may be developed while you are engaged in operations to implement the previously created strategy. Here are four good questions to ask about your strategy (Figure 3-1).

1. Is your strategy long-, medium-, or short-term?
2. What is the degree of risk in each level of strategy?
3. What management approaches are most commonly used in each level of strategy?
4. What alliance structures are most often used in long-, medium-, or short-term strategies?

The figure shows that the risks are generally high in planning long-term strategy. In the United States, this activity, called macro strategy, makes plans for five to fifteen years into the future and involves predictions, external focus, and looking at new processes and markets. A Japanese company's macro-strategy time frame may

Figure 3-1: Strategic Alliances as Component of Long-, Medium-, and Short-Term Corporate Strategy

Risks			
High	**Macro (Long-Term) Strategy—5–15 years**	**Alliance Type**	
	Industry positioning	Equity investment	
	External focus	Acquisition/Diversification	
	Future/Change prediction	technology	
	New processes and technologies	Private/Public partnership	
	New markets	for R&D	
Medium to Low	**Business (Medium-Term) Strategy—2–5 years**	**Alliance Type**	
	Stakeholders	Joint venture	
	(Customers/Suppliers)	Licensing	
	Leadership mgmt. (market share)	Distribution	
	Labor groups	Outsourcing	
	Competitors	Acquisition	
Low	**Operational (Short-Term) Strategy—1–3 years**	**Alliance Type**	
	Financial and asset management	OEM/Private label	
	Product/Market focus	Licensing	
	Resource allocation	Distribution	

© 1990 The Lared Group

be one hundred years. (This is a good example of how strategy is influenced by cultural norms.)

The kind of strategic planning that a company undertakes will affect the nature of the alliances that the company enters into. If a company is willing to undertake long-term strategic planning, the likelihood is very high that the alliances entered into as part of the long-term vision will be those that take some time to come to fruition, such as research and development partnerships, diversifications, and equity investments.

Medium-term strategy—called, simply, business strategy—carries lower risk, owing to its shorter—two to five years—time horizon. It involves stake holders such as customers, suppliers, and labor groups, all influenced by a management perspective that looks to market-share issues. Alliances used commonly as part of medium-term strategy include joint ventures, licensing, distribution, and outsourcing relationships. Most early life-cycle stage companies plan according to this category.

The time frame of short-term, or operational, strategy is one to three years. Managers are looking primarily at financial and asset management with a narrow product and market focus for immediate results. An issue hotly debated in this low-risk part of strategy development is the allocation of resources. Alliances most common here are original equipment manufacture, private label, licensing, and distribution arrangements.

Correlating Strategy with Life-Cycle Stages

An interesting exercise is to correlate the strategy levels shown in Figure 3-1, especially the subset of activities in the "Alliance Type" column to the life-cycle stage of the organization.

Companies in the throes of reinventing themselves through the arrival of a Visionary manager and moving from Declining into Sustaining mode may combine all three levels. The mandate will have been issued by a group of Visionary managers spurred on by a Visionary leader. He and his group will have developed a long-term macro strategy with which to propel the organization forward, and will be working aggressively to develop joint ventures for research and for licensing technology that does not constitute the organization's core competency. These medium- and long-term approaches will include developing spin-off strategies for divisions that do not fit the long-term future positioning of the organization. The short-term strategy will be implemented by a team of managers assembled by the group of Visionary managers to pare down the organization; they will look at operating strategies in order to cut away at redundancy.

Visionary Leadership at Kodak

A real-life example of long-, medium-, and short-term strategies in action was created at Kodak when the Visionary manager George Fisher arrived from Motorola in October 1993.

The hiring of Fisher exemplified a current trend. In the first nine months of 1993, according to Michigan State University Professor Emeritus Eugene E. Jennings, nineteen of sixty-four new CEOs at Fortune 500 industrial companies (31 percent) were outsiders or, in my characterization, Visionary managers brought in to revitalize Mature or Declining companies.

Many outsiders are Visionaries, although it does not necessarily follow that all Visionaries are outsiders. The conventional wisdom is that insiders cannot see beyond the existing culture. Kodak's former CEO, Kay Whitmore, was ousted not because he could not cut costs but because he couldn't change Kodak's style of doing business. Motorola, on the other hand, had a dynamic and flexible culture, and the expectation was that George Fisher would bring that perspective and make the changes necessary to revitalize Kodak. For example, at Motorola Fisher had created the Bandit Team, a highly successful group of employees who had designed, manufactured, and marketed a pager in record time. They were held up as the standard of excellence. That and other similar approaches will be needed to improve upon the current delay in bringing the great technology of Kodak to the market.

As the Visionary manager charged with infusing new life into the company, Fisher has the difficult task of reformulating and safeguarding the long-term strategy of Kodak, while instituting immediate changes in the short- and medium-term approaches. The expectation is that the organization will move, in part at first and then more substantially, into Sustaining, Mature and Consolidating, and possibly (for certain divisions) into Hockeystick modes of operation.

Fisher's most important actions internally have been typical of a Visionary manager. He has refocused the strategy of the company around its imaging business, a core competency, and has created a digital imaging unit, while selling the divisions that specialized in health and household products. He has also boosted morale by outlining the company's bright future and by improving internal communications. Gradually, and not without difficulty, George Fisher is beginning to move the organization into Sustaining mode. His medium- and long-term strategy and its implementation are yet to be revealed and tested in the market.

Unfortunately, like many Visionary managers, Fisher has a limited time in which to prove himself. Cutbacks, layoffs, and restructurings, which have generally already started before the Visionary manager arrives on the scene, all add enormous stress to an organization groaning its way from Declining to Sustaining. Boards of directors of such companies are notoriously impatient for results, looking at two-year time horizons. Fisher must show dramatic results in order to be considered successful.[1]

Small Companies Need Strategies Beyond the Short Term

With small Start-up companies, the process of integrating strategy into the organization is a difficult challenge because of the immediate and crisis-type issues they often face. Generally their approach to strategy, and their consequent interest in alliances, fall under the business strategy or medium-term approach (two to five years). However, many small companies in the Start-up mode are occupied only with short-term planning in the time frame of one to three years. This is consistent with the personalities of Adventurer managers who, though they have a vision, are also impatient and want to see results quickly.

Fulfillment as a Core Competency

Before a small distributor of advanced materials used in the aerospace and electronics industries (a company that I co-owned and operated) could plan its medium- and short-term strategies, the challenge was to discover its core competency. At that time, in 1984, I had no idea that that was the process we were going through, since we were not familiar with the term. We were focused on trying to identify what it was that we did best, a way to differentiate ourselves from our competitors and grow. It was a survival strategy rather than a deft move to reposition the company.

Today, we know that a core competency is an activity or capability in which we, as an organization, are not only better than our competitors, but have a competitive advantage sustainable over time. Our purpose there was to develop a supplier relationship that would enable us to become a better, value-added, lower-cost provider of products to our market.

Our suppliers, mostly multi-billion-dollar conglomerates, were major manufacturers of advanced materials. As a small company we struggled to find a strategy that would make them notice us and give our growing organization preferred treatment. Having large companies as true partners in our growth seemed an impossible dream.

After much rumination and after talking to our customers and most of our major suppliers, we decided that our core competency was in the fulfillment, processing, and customizing of small orders. We had discovered during our analysis that small orders (those under half a million dollars) were, for our larger suppliers, difficult and expensive to fulfill. We, however, thrived on such demands. Based on this examination, we decided upon a medium-term (two to five years) strategy to develop alliance relationships with large suppliers that also sold to a customer base we could not afford to woo. Our idea was to use their muscle to access a segment of the market in which it would otherwise take us years to gain credibility. The benefit to them would be that we could service their smaller customers.

The next challenge was to interest our suppliers in the concept. To our delight, they were pleased and relieved to be able to free themselves of the administrative nightmare of servicing customers who wanted anything from $67.50 worth of titanium dioxide for an experiment to $500,000 worth of thin-film deposition material for aerospace and defense applications—both small orders in their universe. In the short term, their sales representatives would not have to spend time servicing a client where the commission was nonexistent or negligible.

Our services also served their long-term goals. Most of the small-order customers were in the R&D departments of large aerospace and electronics manufacturers. Our suppliers knew that by positioning their company's products and brand name in the research phase of a project's development, they would be assured of being included in the specifications of the projects when these were ultimately put into production. We would protect their brand name and, at the point where the project moved into production and the orders reached a pre-agreed size, we would refer the satisfied customer back to them.

Applying the personality categories explained in Chapter 2, we discovered that the supplier companies all fell into the

Mature and Consolidating stage, whereas our company, although it had been in business for thirty years when we acquired it, had all the characteristics of a Start-up.

By developing this relationship, we reasoned, the Mature suppliers would protect their future market share, and our Start-up organization would grow immediately (short-term), and continue to live and thrive off small-order "crumbs" (medium- and long-term). Both companies would benefit as long as the combination of operational and short-term (us) and macro and long-term (them) strategies was well integrated.

The fact that our potential partners fell into the Mature and Consolidating stage determined our manner of approaching the project. The alliance had to be structured in such a way that it required little attention from the larger partner's senior management. In fact, we knew that once the decision was made to develop a joint distribution relationship with our company, we would be doing most of the work and bearing most of the risk—but also incurring most of the short-term benefit. And the project was definitely a Bet the Farm one for us. So a large amount of effort on our part was appropriate.

Accordingly, our expectations were aligned with the attention (or lack thereof) that we would receive from our partners.

Interestingly enough, one of our partners took the time to learn from us. Their managers were intrigued by the way we serviced our customers. We had an advisory panel of engineers on call to answer knotty research questions in the materials area; one- to two-day turnaround on customized service and delivery; and knowledgeable account executives and order takers. The significance of our partner's behavior is that even the smallest and least important alliances can generate benefits in both directions, if only the partners have a commitment to learn from each other.

One of the key variables we could not foresee was the time it would take for our Mature partners to make the decision to go forward. Since they were complacent, with a proliferation of middle management, we might wait for months for a final decision. Indeed, some of the supplier partners we approached took so long that we went on to the next one before they'd even had the third of *seven* committee meetings we were told would be necessary to discuss our proposal. Needless to say, few of them seemed to have a process for alliance selection and management.

Fortunately, with a couple of companies the decision to develop the relationship was made quickly. These were organizations where individual managerial personality overrode corporate sclerosis. A few managers saw the opportunity and recognized that it was a "win/win" decision, since the project was small from a dollar point of view and their long-term goal was strategically consistent with our short-term strategy. Clearly, there are no guarantees that a Hunter or even a Visionary manager will survive in a company that is in the Mature or even Declining stage, but some do—and we were fortunate enough to have these brave individuals as our internal corporate champions.

For the suppliers the project personality was lower than Experimental, although strategically the protection of their brand name had long-term importance. Remember: Even though an alliance may be of strategic importance, substantial resources may not necessarily be dedicated to it.

"Corporate and alliance strategy" all too often sounds like an exercise that can only be appropriate to or afforded by larger companies. On the contrary, it is indispensable for smaller companies; in fact, it may be impossible for a small or Start-up organization in any industry to go beyond its development stage into Hockeystick or Professional without a strategy that at least reaches from the operational and short-term into the business and medium-term approach.

Short-term thinking (one year) too often characterizes small companies, which are often focused on survival. I know what that feels like. It can be all-consuming. Alliances, however, are by definition relationships that look toward the future. So if you are only focused on the short term, the likelihood is that you will not develop a vision for your organization, and will miss opportunities for growth, especially those offered by alliances.

The Global Strategic Plan

Developing a global strategic plan is an intricate process, and is not the subject matter of this book. However, its relationship to the area of alliances is critical, since some international opportunities may be leveraged only by using the alliance process and learning the skills of managing cross-cultural alliances. In the domestic marketplace, some companies can decide to avoid the alliance process as a growth or diversification option, but in the international arena, the need for local expertise, cultural interpreters, and the legal and political ramifications of entering foreign markets will virtually mandate the development of partnerships and alliances of all kinds.*

If the company is global, or even transnational, it is fair to assume that its strategic plan will be globally developed. For those readers who are not familiar with the process of developing a global strategic plan, the approach includes some elements common to all strategic planning: the description of the business and its activities, its positioning for the future (which involves an analysis of key competitors, both visible and invisible, worldwide), and the financial goals of the organization. In addition, all of the above are analyzed regionally. The way this analysis is compiled globally is by

* These issues are handled in my course "Managing Globally." See page 236 for details.

having country or regional managers contribute information on a per-country basis. Only the most strategically important country/markets contribute. The collection of this information is facilitated by a cross-functional team of managers, often those who head the various business units in major regions worldwide.

For companies involved in this process the decision as to which countries to focus on is a difficult one. A global strategic approach requires considering not only countries that have present importance but also those that may have future importance—for instance, China.

For many organizations, the vastness of the Chinese market has immediate and future strategic importance. If investigation and entry into China is not included in a strategic plan (which could include an alliance strategy), positioning and market share could be lost in the future. The political and economic risks are considerable. Nevertheless, the strategic plan must balance the risks of not entering with those of doing so. The implementation plan for that strategy, which may include alliances, could suggest entering the China market through a Taiwanese, a Japanese, or a Hong Kong (perhaps higher-risk in the light of 1997) partnership.

If the strategic plan of a company operating internationally is not global in its analysis, alliances that could make sense for the future may never be considered.

A combination of approaches is useful in creating a global strategic plan. They involve analyzing inputs from strategic regions, combining that with a competitive analysis, and developing a strategy that will have a "bottom-up" genesis, meaning that operating managers who are familiar with local and regional conditions will contribute their practical input and experience and also know their concerns were integrated. Such a plan is more likely to be well implemented than "top-down" plans. Clearly, many companies include as part of their global strategic plan the alliance process and opportunity.

The Global Strategic Plan and the Alliance Plan

The place for global strategic discussions is at the strategic planning stage—not when a plan is considered for a specific alliance. Alliance planning is a subset of strategic planning and must follow that process. However, the two functions must be interrelated, otherwise inconsistencies will occur in the regions chosen and the partners selected.

Be wary of proactive potential partners that may throw your strategic direction off course. An opportunistic partner may cause your company to move in a strategic direction that is contrary to your corporate goals. Regardless of the excitement of the chase, recognize that they may not be a true strategic fit and resist the temptation. Do not try to squeeze a nonstrategic partner into a strategic fit.

There are, however, situations where a proactive partner could provide a fresh direction that is desirable. You may decide that a particular opportunity is exciting enough for you to change parts of your plan. But realize that that is what is happening. The point here is to question, analyze, and address that opportunity with the same intensity and care that is brought to the strategic planning process, so as to integrate the new direction.

As an entrepreneur, I found that planning did not come easily to me. But I have learned that hasty decisions about alliances almost always turn out poorly. The planning process can be visualized as three layers (see Figure 3-2).

Time Is Your Friend

Time works in your favor in alliance development. It takes on average six months to create a domestic alliance and much longer for international ones. Time teaches you how your partner will behave under a variety of circumstances. Market conditions such as rapidly changing product life cycles, the need for secrecy, and the difficulty of keeping relationship development confidential could force an acceleration of alliance creation. You will work with those constraints and do what must be done. But I counsel as a general rule that there is good reason not to rush the process, since it is just that, a process, and the more issues that can be raised, lived with, discussed, debated, and resolved, the better the working relationship will be later on.

Organizations that focus on acquisitions as their main alliance structure will be tempted to focus on deal closure. They will have a tendency to push, to hurry, to score only on closure. In such organizations, internal reporting may be described in terms of numbers of companies acquired or deals signed, with less emphasis on ongoing issues of integration and implementation.

Planning the alliance properly may draw out the time it takes to enter the exhilarating part of alliance development, when the partners are courting each other and individual managers see glory and career enhancement glowing in their futures. Be patient! You'll achieve greater success in the long run if you take it slowly in the beginning.

Figure 3-2: The Planning Process

Looking at Options

Analyzing options involves decisions on strategy, philosophy, corporate personality, and structure. The kinds of questions that should be asked include the following:

- Why are we looking at an alliance now?
- What do we want to achieve from the alliance?
- Is an alliance the best way for us to achieve our goals?
- What resources are we willing to commit to this relationship?
- How is our company most comfortable in the creation of alliance relationships?
- How much control are we willing to cede to an alliance partner?

This discussion should involve more than just top management. Input from various functions within the organization will be valuable, providing insights that could change a strategy—for example, from acquisition to licensing—if the answers to these questions indicate that the goals of the company can be better achieved in that way. Operating managers frequently scoff at the structure that was chosen for an alliance by those at corporate headquarters. They ask, "Why did we acquire this company when we could have obtained their technology by licensing it?" Involving operations-level managers in every stage of the discussion will prevent such negative postmortems.

Sometimes posing the simple question "Why are we looking for an alliance?" to those in marketing, finance, R&D, and sales as well as corporate will yield four or five very different answers. The reasons could include: to expand the product life cycle, to increase the depth of a product line, to increase the market share domestically or internationally, to add new technology, to reduce costs, or to divest a business. Clarifying these options, listing and examining them, is all part of the discipline that will force you to think proactively about strategically appropriate actions.

Then you must prioritize the options by having the various interested parties within the company list them in order of preference or importance, so that there is an understanding of the reasons for alliance development. The managers in the operating division who will have the responsibility for implementing and managing the alliance and will be answerable for its profit or loss need to have a say in the philosophy and structure chosen for the alliance. You may find that there is some disagreement on the organization's priorities and you will be able to see what approaches are consistent with your organization's corporate personality.

Finally, once your options are chosen and prioritized, they must be related to the organization's strategy as seen in the long-, medium-, or short-term plan. The basic premise of this options analysis is that the possibility is open of choosing an option different from the one considered previously. Keep in mind the macro changes taking place in the global community in the present and future. This may be the time to choose an option that will give you cost-effective local market access and the ability to leverage your core skills. Implementing this may include outsourcing your non-critical capabilities: taking the activities of your company that do not fall within the definition of core competency, looking for alliance partners for whom the activities are their core competencies, and contracting with them to perform those services for you.

In summary, your options analysis should follow these steps:

1. Consider whether you should be looking for an alliance, and if so, why. Get answers from people in different functions in the company.
2. List, discuss, and prioritize the reasons, and reach a consensus.
3. Identify the options for alliance structures, using the Pyramid of Alliances. Consider cost, risk, and the commitment of human resources.
4. Focus on specific structures with an understanding of your organization's corporate personality. For example, your cor-

porate personality may require complete control rather than collaborative team building. If so, acquisition may be the right level of the Pyramid of Alliances for you.

5. Relate choices to corporate strategy and strategic plan, and test for consistency.

If this process generates some solid options, you will be ready to move to the next series of investigations, Corporate Self-analysis, discussed in Chapter 4. The aim of Chapter 4 is to help you answer the question: Once you know why you want to enter an alliance, how do you do it?

4.
Corporate
Self-Analysis

Corporate Self-Analysis is the task of examining your own company—its cultural characteristics and practices, its financial and managerial strengths and weaknesses, and its strategic direction—before developing plans for the possible use of alliances in pursuit of company goals.

Some companies get stuck at this point. Corporate Self-Analysis is an unfamiliar, even uncomfortable, process for many firms. As a result, many companies bypass this activity, which should be undertaken at the beginning of the alliance-planning process, and then find later that mistakes can be traced back to inadequate understanding of their own organizational motives and behaviors that are rewarded or sanctioned within their organization. It takes effort and commitment as well as an open attitude to develop an understanding and analysis of our corporate cultures. Unless we understand how we do things, both good practices and bad, we will have great difficulty in finding the right partner and then in managing the relationship. It is much more difficult and risky to wait to do the self-analysis when you're already sitting at the negotiating table or in the throes of resolving an ongoing partnership conflict.

I suggest the use of a cross-functional team of people from various parts of the organization to develop the self-analysis. In a global, transnational, or exporter culture, the questions must be answered from the perspectives of executives in various country cultures. You may be surprised to find out that the organization does not have a consistent or uniform approach to address the issues that are raised by the analysis. If your company's practices are confusing for executives within your own organization, imagine how much difficulty a partner will have in dealing with these issues.

Corporate Self-Analysis is not the same as the global strategic plan process. It's a much more intimate—in privately held companies, at times even personal—examination of issues that are not often raised. The garnering of that information, the way the discussions are facilitated, and the freedom and career safety that participants must feel to contribute enthusiastically to the process will determine whether the exercise is useful or a mere formality.

When I do this kind of soul searching with both for-profit and not-for-profit organizations, I take the groups involved off-site, and I constantly emphasize that the environment is nonjudgmental. I mix the group up so that different functions within the company intermingle—research with sales, marketing with finance and so on. These people may rarely speak to one another in ordinary circumstances. It's very helpful for them to hear other points of view.

The Corporate Self-analysis process focuses on the elements of your company's profile, each of which is discussed in this chapter:

   I. The Culture Cluster
  II. The Financial Picture
 III. The Business Definition and SWOT Analysis
 IV. The Possible Strategic Direction

I. The Culture Cluster

Organizations develop a belief system about reality, value, honesty, and reward and punishment in much the same way that a country's society develops a national culture. A corporate or organizational culture is a set of coping mechanisms, or adaptation skills, that members of the culture use both within and outside their corporate environment. Of course, company cultures normally exist within national cultures: The company culture can be seen as the micro culture and the country's as the macro culture.

The corporate culture manifests itself in a variety of corporate habit patterns, often seen in the form of rituals. In fact, one of the overriding values of Declining organizations is that they have institutionalized ritualistic behavior. For example, every new idea is sent to a task force which essentially destroys it; or, memo distribution is excessive with copies going to people for internal political reasons only. Companies in other stages of the life cycle all have their own peculiarities; for example, modes of dress vary by industry and level of entrepreneurship, and of course, country culture.

The way people relax together in a corporate environment also reveals a lot about its culture. Many companies have sports teams and different departments compete against each other. Friday casual dress day is another company cultural norm. Yet apparent informality can be deceiving. In an earlier phase of my career I was a new associate lawyer in a large law firm. The annual firm party was one in which everyone supposedly let their defenses down. However, the hierarchy of power remained intact—which initially confused us new associates, since everyone encouraged us to "relax" and "have a good time." We soon discovered that senior partners expected to receive the same reverence and respect that they were accorded in the office, regardless of how relaxed we might feel. They remembered if one was too familiar—which would be a factor much later when it came time for the associate's review. Generally, larger firms usually fall into the Mature and Consolidating and the Declining categories. They have more rigid cultures.

As new employees of a company we learn these norms on a daily basis. The process is accelerated if we have a mentor. Strategic partners, however, have no way of understanding the myriad unwritten rules of how business is done in our organizations, unless they are particularly observant. Understanding the benefits or the difficulties presented by these unwritten cultural rules will accelerate the learning your organization wants to transfer, and curtail that which it does not, while allowing compromise on cultural clashes where necessary.

The Culture Cluster can be divided into ten separate areas that should be examined. These ten factors are interrelated and sometimes overlap. At the very least you should use the Culture Cluster to understand your own organization. At best, when a possible partner is being considered seriously, use these questions to understand their culture. The Culture Cluster analysis is an acceptable exercise for most potential partners, especially if it is placed in the context of understanding the implementation milestones that will be acceptable within their culture and compatible with yours.

The ten factors that each company should look at as the first step of Corporate Self-Analysis are the following:

1. Styles of decision making and problem solving
2. Authority—delegation and control; reporting methods
3. Work behavior
4. Compensation and incentives
5. Leadership and mentoring styles
6. Communication—oral; written; nonverbal
7. Levels of secrecy
8. Attitude toward time and milestones

9. Ethics and values
10. Personal versus corporate goals

The investigation of each of these factors will vary in intensity or depth with your organizational personality as well as that of your partner. The more you know about these characteristics, the better you will be able to anticipate different styles and management responses to changes in the partnership fortunes.

Let's look at each factor more closely.

1. Decision Making and Problem Solving

This covers all the ways decisions are made in an organization, including those that reflect management and board receptivity to new ideas, especially the alliance concept. This is one of the most common areas for culture clash in alliances. One decision-making style is the "shoot from the hip," haphazard decision-making style of some Start-up companies, where there is no real strategic plan, or, if there is a plan, it is changed at the whim of the company founder when an idea comes up that appears more expedient.

Some Hockeystick companies still have the "shoot from the hip" characteristic. The problem can be exacerbated in that stage because sales revenues are accelerating and it's difficult to argue with success. But the company may run into a brick wall when everyone in the organization defers to the Warrior manager, and makes no decision without the Warrior's approval.

Revolving-Door Management at a Hockeystick Company

"Shoot-from-the-hip" management plagues one company in the retail clothing business, a firm so recognizable that every teenager in the United States and much of the rest of the world wants to drape themselves in the company's products. Unfortunately, although new senior and experienced management have been recruited into the company over the past year, few of them have stayed. Revolving-door management is becoming a characteristic of this Hockeystick organization, since all real decision making continues to reside with the founder-owner, regardless of the lip service paid to planning, strategy, and systems.

The company culture is solidly set. It will take a down-turn—caused either by an aggressive competitive challenge or a refocusing of the market—to change it.

The decision-making analysis should examine senior-to-senior and senior-to–middle managerial processes. These are the individuals who will most likely be involved in an alliance. If you have done the options analysis, you will have an idea of the areas in which you will be looking for alliances—say, distribution or research and development—and the functional areas that would be affected by such alliances.

Let's say, the vice president of business development (a staff, not a line or operating function) is involved in the initial stage of finding an alliance. In this case, her decision-making relationship with operating managers (who will actually manage the alliance) as well as with the executives senior to her is important to understand. Operating managers within the partner company would want to be sure they understand the level of authority of such an executive, and how her decisions would relate to the line of business and to operating managers who would ultimately have to be responsible for implementing the alliance.

Obtaining this information from a potential partner is difficult. Sometimes one can obtain direct information from a potential partner by asking directly, "What is the decision-making process within your organization?" Whatever the answer, the information gathered has to be verified indirectly by observing how authority is given to one manager rather than another, or how certain managers make some decisions but defer to more senior managers for others. Body language as well as direct verbal information can be invaluable in discerning the real holder of decision-making power, as opposed to those who have impressive titles but are not the real decision makers.

If the alliance project is to be within a specific functional area, like R&D, the analysis of the decision-making factor in Corporate Self-analysis might focus on how a project director in research would be empowered in a joint R&D venture, and how she would relate to the director and vice president of research in terms of milestone approval or project changes.

An important aspect of decision making is conflict resolution. By this I don't mean calling in the lawyers. The issue here is the facilitation and solution-finding process, which generally involves finding compromises. Does the organization have a conflict-resolution process in place that sends an issue to a more senior executive or a committee? If not, how are problems resolved? Through memo writing? Committee meetings? One-on-one communications? Documenting this information will not only assist you in understanding and communicating your cultural preferences to partners, but can also be helpful in educating members of the alliance team when it is formed. Some managers may be ignorant of the unwritten rules of their own firm's corporate culture.

Another issue that frequently arises, especially in venture-backed companies, is that of board receptivity. In Chapter 6 we'll examine a case history of a company where the ostensible decision-making power resided in senior management but actual power remained with the board. Venture-capital investors have motivations that are vastly different from those in family-owned or publicly held companies. Awareness of these motivations must become an explicit part of the culture for managers who are developing alliances and need to understand their venture shareholder issues and goals.

For the above and many other reasons relating to effective management of the alliance in the future, as well as selection of a compatible partner in the present, it is essential that you understand how your organization makes decisions. Then, when a potential partner arrives on the scene, you will be able to align their managers' expectations with your reality. And your managers will attempt to do the same with their organization.

2. Authority—Delegation and Control; Reporting Methods

In part, the decision-making analysis will naturally raise issues concerning authority. Focusing specifically on this area, you must ask, "How is authority delegated and what management controls are in place, including reporting responsibilities?" What we want to discover here is not only the official organization chart, but also the actual one. Again, the focus should be on the functional areas that would be involved in or affected by an alliance, which will have been discovered in the options analysis.

3. Work Behavior

The topic of work behavior comprises dress, management of work space, arrival and departure norms, and whether a company is task- or process-oriented. Many high-tech companies are known for their flexible work hours. One Start-up company involved in speech recognition was actually more productive at night than during the daylight hours. At three in the morning there were more than a hundred programmers in the building and the place was bustling with activity. Other organizations use time cards to regulate and record the comings and goings of all employees. Corporate life-cycle stages will have a bearing on employee work behavior, as will industry types. Start-up and Hockeystick companies, along with certain Professional ones, will evidence longer work hours, more flexibility, and more casual dress. The Mature and Consolidating, Declining, and Sustaining companies will generally be more formal. An example is the IBM corporate uniform of well-tailored suit, white shirt, and tie, and formal clean-cut looks, also seen in the conservative dress of many large consulting and law firms. (In some divisions of the "new" IBM, the once-sacrosanct conservative look has now given way to a studiedly casual look.)

The legal profession is notorious for long work hours. Many large firms, especially in securities, corporate finance, or litigation, are as busy on the weekends as they are during the week. Entrepreneurial law firms and companies of all kinds exhibit Start-up characteristics and generally have enormous flexibility as to when the work gets done—the main issue is that it does get done on time or in advance—that is, yesterday.

Macro, or country, cultures also influence certain work habits, some of which may be related to the weather. The heat of the day in southern Europe, Mexico, some Latin American countries, and the Middle East may call for a long hiatus in the midday hours. Another aspect of work styles that greatly affects an international alliance relationship is the philosophical question of "living to work" or "working to live."★

Work-space design is an important indication of culture. We Americans assume that with increasing authority goes more lavish work space. Don't be deceived by crowded work spaces, as in some Asian countries. The macro or country culture may call for close working quarters. This does not necessarily indicate lack of authority.

Law-firm work-space design in the 1970s and 1980s reflected the expansive nature of that industry. Even though downsizing has changed the space layout somewhat, big corner offices and ornateness of decor still abound in the profession as they do in the investment-banking world.

The messages communicated to a potential strategic partner by the physical environment of your organization may be different from the ones you give them verbally. This analysis will make you aware of any potential discrepancies in order to explain them if necessary.

4. Compensation and Incentives

Most organizations have standard policies and procedures regarding compensation and incentives. The problems occur when an alliance

★ These issues are handled in my course "Managing Globally." See page 236 for details.

might call for a company to find a different way of looking at compensation. One company encountered a cultural clash when an entrepreneurial partner with whom they were in an international alliance suggested an incentive system that included a phantom stock plan. Both the country (macro) and corporate (micro) cultures ran against this idea. If just the micro culture had been the problem, the issue might have been able to be resolved.

Another client encountered a problem in a distribution agreement when their sales representatives were offered different incentives from the partner's. In addition, the two companies had not thought through the issues that could arise in the sales and service relationships. Who would get the commission and credit? Where were the geographic or product delineations to be drawn? Who got to service the customer relationship and to whom did the account belong? The details of the reward, compensation, and incentive systems had the power to destroy a strategically important relationship. Again, a clear statement of understanding of the corporate culture regarding this issue in the inception stages of relationship planning would have averted the bad feelings and diminishment of trust that later were very difficult to repair.

5. Leadership and Mentoring Styles

Leadership styles are often related to stages in the corporate life cycle, and so become a natural part of a cultural analysis. As a general rule, the kind of manager attracted to a company in a certain stage of its company's life cycle will exhibit a style that is acceptable in that corporate culture. Leadership styles (a subset of personality traits) can vary from autocratic (exerting total control) to totally delegative (exerting little or no control). The amount of leader control is inversely proportional to the amount of group participation. Clearly, at the autocratic level there is no group participation. Some country cultures are much more comfortable with that leadership style than others. In certain parts of India a good business leader will be one who makes decisions without asking for the input of his subordinates. Asking for collaboration, as most American managers do, would be seen as a sign of weakness, a lack of knowledge and authority, or at worst as incompetence.

By contrast, a U.S. Hunter manager in a Professional company will focus on encouraging collaborative decision making. Subordinates are often delegated authority to make a variety of important decisions and are empowered to institute change within previously discussed and negotiated guidelines. Nordstrom's, a retail department store, has as its entire employee mandate a five-by-eight-inch card with one rule: "Use your good judgment in all situations."[1]

Start-up companies in all cultures are an interesting mixture. They range from highly collaborative to highly autocratic—even to the extent of the development of a "personality cult," if a founder is particularly brilliant: He will often be imitated in his dress (even down to his choice of glasses frame design), speech characteristics, and personal mannerisms. Thus, although the leadership style may appear participative, the culture really only accepts carbon copies of the leader's ideas and style, often with great short-term success. Such a style can encounter difficulties when competitive or market changes require a different mind-set. At that point an outsider, a Hunter manager with Professional skills, may be needed to change and systematize the organization's processes.

Michael Dell—From Adventurer to Hunter

Some managers have the unusual ability to change their characteristics with the growth cycles of their organizations. One such manager is Michael Dell, founder and CEO of Dell Computer Corporation.

Dell was the classic Adventurer manager when I first met him. He was twenty years old then and had already started to build a successful company. In the intervening years he has grown with his organization from Adventurer to Warrior and now is migrating into the area of Hunter manager.

This is due in no small part to the influence of mentors such as George Kozmetsky, the cofounder of Teledyne, Inc., and others. This perspective, combined with the passage of time and experience, has expanded Dell's horizons on management, while he has kept his unique vision of the industry and of his company.

Mentoring at Apple

A number of companies have made well-integrated mentoring programs an important part of their management style. Apple Computer is one of them. The company chooses individuals steeped in organizational culture to groom others who are less familiar with the culture. Mentoring provides political and substantive internal access for fast-track junior executives.

Apple Computer's corporate commitment to mentoring has evolved over time. Now the organization is looking particularly to the issues of making their employees competitive for the future and designing internal leadership programs that enhance the careers of individuals, especially in the global market. Under their mentoring program fast-track executives who are nominated by the management of various divisions are given the opportunity to spend one year working closely with a corporate mentor. The executive-in-training must be seen as having high potential in a variety of categories of performance so that the company's significant investment will pay off.

Mentors are knowledgeable about Apple internal politics and are able to communicate the unwritten culture of Apple as well as any opportunities for advancement available. According to Denise Coley, the strategic program business manager with the Advanced Technology Group at Apple Computer and the designer of the mentoring program, "The

> formal mentoring program gives the opportunity for career advancement to many different individuals, which informal mentoring may not do. If an alliance manager is involved in a mentoring program, you will know that he has access to those who can assist him to navigate some of the covert ways of corporate decision making."[2]

Understanding both mentoring and leadership styles will give you and your partner good information about the importance, access, and internal approval capabilities of the managers involved in the alliance. Looking out for these qualities and criteria in your partner will give you better insight as to the internal power and influence of the corporate champion on the project. It may also alert you to any power-structure changes in your partner that could potentially endanger your joint project.

6. Communication—Oral; Written; Nonverbal

Earlier the executive in a Declining company was mentioned whose policy was that anyone wanting a phone conversation with him first had to write a letter. Memo writing, very common in Mature and Declining companies, is a political and self-protective tool. It is also a delaying mechanism that can forestall the necessity of making a decision under the pretext of the "need for further research." In this way, the message being communicated is not the one written down; rather, the act itself causes the delay, shelves the project, and avoids risk—and risk avoidance is the real message.

It is very difficult to analyze communication methods in a Declining organization. The very act of Corporate Self-Analysis requires a capacity for corporate self-examination—but this capacity is not one of the traits of such a culture. On the contrary, the culture encourages a "there's nothing wrong here" approach, letting people metaphorically move the deck chairs around while the ship is sinking.

Can We Talk Without Overheads?

One group of executives from an aerospace company laughed for a long time when we started discussing this issue. The reason was that their company culture was so ingrained that they hadn't even thought about how they handle written communication as a trait. But it became clear that one of the issues that they had with an outside partner for a research project was the way they presented information to each other.

The aerospace company executives never made presentations without viewgraphs presented on an overhead projector. Their partner saw no need for that nicety and wanted to have discussions, with only some minor handouts, whenever they met. The aerospace company couldn't make decisions unless the material was presented in a way with which they felt comfortable. Their perception was that the partner was sloppy and unprepared and didn't give the project serious enough attention. They also misread the cultural difference and saw the communication issues as substantive problems, which they were not.

Country (macro) culture is of course important in communications. Miscommunications can occur on many levels when you combine country cultures, beliefs, systems, values, protocol, and traditions. For example, the extent to which disagreement and open discussion are encouraged or discouraged varies from culture to culture, both country and corporate. Leadership styles vary in close relationship to the degree of openness in discussions. If a Mature and Consolidating company does not encourage frank discussion of differences, problems will go underground but will not go away. Couple such a company with a Hockeystick partner where everyone speaks their mind, and you will see the sparks fly.

There is a similar lack of congruity between a Warrior manager, with his confrontative and aggressive style and the Farmer, well entrenched with his Old Boy network and complacent management group. The two may well conflict if forced to work together; the Warrior may be seen as a renegade, and may antagonize his partner management group so much that conflict becomes unresolvable.

When managing an alliance, understanding the differences in communication styles helps to lessen the tension. But the real struggle occurs at an earlier point, in the planning stage. If you cannot conquer your organizational reluctance to analyze this issue now, it may come back to haunt you later when you are already invested in a partnership.

7. Levels of Secrecy

Closely related to communication, the level of secrecy considered necessary also follows the continuum of the life-cycle stages, with Start-up companies generally being most open. The exception to this is that family or closely privately held companies are often very secretive, no matter what stage of the cycle they are in. This law of secrecy applies to revealing corporate goals, knowing who the actual decision makers are, closed-door meetings, etc. Often, employees create an in-group, who knows the answers, and an out-group, who doesn't. Of course, public companies cannot be secretive about the information that must be disclosed by law. However, that does not mean that internally and politically they are open. Many Politician managers in Declining organizations have perfected the secretive and personal self-protective style that keeps them in office.

The most extreme mismatch is that of an Adventurer manager in combination with a later-phase company. The Adventurer manager in the Start-up is rarely equipped to navigate the paths of power in some Mature and Consolidating and most Declining companies, especially with reference to the issue of secrecy. In a partnership with such a company, the Adventurer may have a very short fuse. For example, he may be told that the person with whom he is dealing is the decision maker, and his expectations for getting speedy responses will rise correspondingly. His frustrations will mount as he is confronted with the necessity for constant reselling of every step in the alliance process to new players who appear on the partner's team. This makes him suspicious and destroys his trust, especially if it continues to occur after he has been involved in the alliance process for some time. As a first step, it is critical to understand how the openness/secrecy issue is handled in your company in order to develop a process that will be able to work in an alliance that includes an Adventurer.

The next step is communicating that knowledge to your partner. The third step, which is discussed in Chapter 6, is to create a "fast-track" communication mechanism and environment that effects a micro-cultural change. That will mean that the alliance communications are now open within a certain organizational group and for a defined set of projects, and the secretive style is avoided in order to facilitate an alliance between a later-stage company and an Adventurer, Warrior, or Professional manager.

Politician managers will be very reluctant to examine this issue. Farmer managers, who are fairly complacent, will also resist the process. Visionary managers, on the other hand, will face it head-on and force the closed-door meetings into the open.

8. Attitude Toward Time and Milestones

Individuals, companies, and countries, differ enormously in their conceptions of time. "On time" to one may be "half an hour late" to another. This issue has particular impact where decision making is multilayered. Time is a cultural norm. The terms "now," "soon," and "on time" have a corporate cultural meaning and sometimes a vastly different macro-cultural one as well. Start-up companies have a sense of urgency, so "now" means "today," if not "this minute." A Start-up company in the Netherlands would temper that urgency to include some consensus building, so "now" could mean "tomorrow." In a Mature and Consolidating company in the Netherlands that consensus building could take months, even years. Milestones have to do with the time-related expectations that are placed within and around alliance projects. Some cultures believe in the natural progression of activities, i.e. "We cannot externally control them." Those cultures, Saudi Arabia for example, will resist aggressive pushing for specific time-related milestones, focusing rather on the multifaceted aspects of relationship development.

Speedcom Time Versus Judge Time

At a program on international management skills at a major computer company, Speedcom,* the talk was scheduled to begin at 9:00 A.M. A number of executives wandered in at 9:05, more at 9:10, and hundreds around 9:15. I started at 9:20. According to the organizer of the program, we had begun the program "on time." What she meant was that in Speedcom time, a twenty-minute delay in start time was the corporate norm.

How vastly different that was from the situation when I clerked for a superior court judge. Lawyers had to be in his court at 7:29 A.M. for a 7:30 start time, when the judge would call the cases for the day in rapid succession. If you were not there to answer when your name was called, he would "continue" (that is, postpone) the case, putting it off sometimes for months, and causing all sorts of problems for clients and opposing counsel. I called it "judge" time. He was relentless. As you can imagine, his court was one of the most efficient in the district. He set the cultural rules; everyone knew and lived by them or suffered the consequences.

Members of alliances can experience continuing frustrations resulting from time-related cultural differences. It is critical to un-

* Not the company's real name.

derstand your own corporate norms in this area and to communicate them to your partners in the language and terms that fit with their cultural understandings.

One senior executive of a Mature company confided, "We told them [the alliance partners] up front that 'now' meant in three or four weeks. They laughed and thought we were joking. I reminded them again later when I received an irate phone call from the CEO of what I now realize was a Hockeystick company. He just couldn't understand why it would take us so long to make a decision when the result would be an almost immediate sales increase. Now it was my turn to laugh. I recognized him as a Warrior, whose focus was revenues above all. I explained that 'now' was a cultural norm. It was nothing personal nor did it indicate a lack of interest in the project. He didn't like it—but he understood."

9. Ethics and Values

Ethics has become a hot topic in the 1990s. An extensive subject in its own right, it can be handled here only in passing. It is, however, worthy of mention because the issue of differing ethics has been raised a number of times in the context of problem alliances. In a recent discussion, the CEO of a multi-billion-dollar company confided that ethics was the real issue behind most of the difficulties that he and his organization were having in one of their partnerships. The CEO of the partner, a high-profile, headline-grabbing businessman, was an aggressive Warrior whose success was legendary. When the alliance was announced, the multi-billion-dollar company saw its stock jump considerably. But the reality was that the partner's tactics involved unethical behavior—not illegal, but unethical.

Of course each of us has an individual code of ethics, be it based on the Judeo-Christian or another of the world religions, or on a nonreligious code such as humanism. But how will you know what is unethical for your company unless you've addressed the issue? In a corporate environment, until recently, ethical codes were mostly unwritten. Now, fortunately, many organizations are actively developing a code of ethics.

Don't underestimate the importance of ethics. Ethical attitudes permeate the entire culture; people with similar beliefs are attracted to each other, whereas those with a different code of ethics will gravitate elsewhere. The purpose of this evaluation is not to sit in moral judgment of others—although at times it's difficult not to express opinions when you see unethical behavior. The goal is to understand the code under which you are operating and, likewise, your partner.

Ethics is influenced greatly by the country (macro) cultures in which you operate. Economically emerging countries are especially ethically challenging to highly industrialized and knowledge-based cultures, mostly found in the West. This is because what Western cultures consider "bribery," other cultures consider a normal way and cost of doing business. Conversely, our willingness in the West, and especially in the United States, to downsize long-term and loyal employees to achieve stockholder returns, is seen as an unethical violation of a strongly held social contract among members of a community and a society, by those in other cultures such as Germany, Sweden, mainland China and, despite some recent layoffs, Japan.

A recent *Business Week* article[3] discussed the stages whereby "frontier capitalism" evolves into democratized capitalism, an analysis that explains the different perceptions of ethics and why doing business in other, especially emerging, cultures can be so difficult for Westerners.

Stage 1, after statist economies collapse, could be called the Age of Corruption. The black market thrives, and the activities of pirates, gangsters, and extortionists experience explosive growth and these groups expand their influence.

In Stage 2 family businesses begin to develop; often very small, they are fiercely independent and entrepreneurial. As this group grows, they establish some rules of commerce. The legal system, although weak and without meaningful enforcement mechanisms, begins to evolve. The United States was in Stage 2 during the age of the robber barons like Cornelius Vanderbilt, who rose from wharf rat to shipping magnate in New York City. He once wrote to associates who had seized one of his properties: "Gentlemen, you have undertaken to cheat me. I will not sue you, for the law takes too long. I will ruin you."

In Stage 3 economic growth is accelerating but difficult to measure. Financial markets begin to evolve and some foreign institutional investors enter the market. The legal code matures.

Russia in the mid-1990s is clearly in Stage 1. Judy Shelton, an economist at the Hoover Institution at Stanford University quoted in the above-mentioned article, is optimistic that Russia will evolve soon into Stage 2. "It will become a comparative advantage to become honest and to honor contracts," she predicts. For some companies already active in Russia, the sooner the better.

My own observation as an international businessperson is that there are two further stages. In Stage 4 the economy has evolved to the point of attaining the Western mode of commerce and economic behavior with which we are so familiar. Stage 5, however, is where legal institutions and procedures are so constraining that the system no longer works. Government regulations stultify entrepreneurship and risk taking, and legal remedies tend to benefit the perpetrators and the guilty, while harming the innocent and the victimized. In short, the system turns itself on its head. In this stage, gangs and major criminal enterprises (for example, the illegal drug industry) benefit from the gridlock of law enforcement and government owing to conflict between the rights of an individual and the protection of society. It appears that in the United States we are in Stage 4 but evolving to Stage 5.

Ethics is the topic that has always preoccupied philosophers, economists, and ethicists. It is important to raise the issue as part of the Culture Cluster analysis because ethics has come up with increasing frequency as an alliance deal breaker in recent years. For example, one U.S.-China joint venture in Shanghai encountered fatal conflict when bribes, characterized as "fees," were demanded. Under U.S. law, the U.S. partner was prevented from paying. The Chinese partner was unwilling to proceed. Planning for added costs or realities of doing business in jurisdictions where such practices are common may continue to cause difficulties for companies unwilling or unable to incorporate such practices. For others, relying on a local partner to handle these matters may be an acceptable alternative. I recommend you take this into consideration in your alliance-planning process. Your ethical position as an organization will clarify the decisions that you must make when you balance business opportunity with ethical decisions made in selecting a compatible partner.

10. Personal Versus Corporate Goals

To what extent do personal and company goals overlap? The final aspect of the Culture Cluster is of particular importance in family-owned companies. The family goals may make perfect sense to the family, because of historical issues and relationship matters, but to the general business community they could appear peculiar or illogical. If the company is privately held, the family will have no reason to share their intimate concerns with others. In this case, the personal goals of the family *are* the corporate ones and they may be unclear to anyone in the entire organization except the family members. In an alliance with a family-owned company, the other partner needs to understand the family way of doing things, especially if it isn't rational from a business perspective.

This matter must be handled with great tact, but firmly, when one is working with family-held businesses. The cultural analysis can be done on a "need to know basis"; one-on-one discussions with key family members can elucidate corporate actions and direction. Too often this is not done, owing to secrecy or neglect— no one thought to ask the questions. And it can destroy an existing partnership or prevent a new one from happening.

Family Ties Down Under

A client firm approached us to assist them in the selection of a strategic acquisition. They had already made the determination that the acquisition structure was the one that best fit their culture. (Actually, they'd not considered any other structure, but culturally they felt they had no other option.) The company was a multi-billion-dollar U.S. company in the industrial chemicals business on an expansion rampage. Now they wanted entry into the Australian market.

An aside: I characterize their activities as an "expansion rampage" because today, four years later, under the leadership of a new CEO, they are divesting themselves of many of their ill-thought-out acquisitions as aggressively as they originally acquired them—classic behavior for Hockeystick companies that move through the Professional into the Mature stage, and need to consolidate.

We approached our consulting associate in Australia. He took the corporate partner criteria that we had jointly developed with the client and found what appeared to be the perfect acquisition. It was a family-owned company involving a father and three sons, and they were interested.

At that point our client indicated that they applied the same strategy to all their acquisitions and knew exactly what they had to do. Although we suggested they analyze the potential partnership carefully, considering cultural and other differences, our advice went unheeded, and the Warrior CEO barreled ahead. He boarded his private jet with his senior management team and took off for Australia.

The first meeting with the smaller company went well. They were well run, efficient, courteous, and hospitable. The Warrior took his team back to the United States and began the due diligence process: verifying financial and legal information on the company. They didn't want our Australian partner's input, nor would they listen to our advice, offered again, that they modify their approach to take into account cultural differences.

They boarded the jet once again and went back Down Under with an offer. It was turned down. The U.S. Warrior recrunched the numbers and rationalized that his original offer could certainly be negotiated upward. He made a second offer. It, too, was turned down. Annoyed, the Warrior CEO refused to go any further.

We met. He complained that the Australians had an inflated opinion of the value of their company. I offered to have our Australian partner investigate. Our partner in Sydney belonged to the same club as the owner of the Australian company—the community is well interconnected in a country with a relatively small population. They met over eighteen holes and a couple of beers.

"We thought they were a good company, they seem reputable enough," the Australian CEO told our partner. "The problem is that they keep offering us more money."

Our partner listened attentively. "The problem isn't money, is it?" he added encouragingly.

The Australian CEO nodded. "Of course not. We've made a mint in the past. The real issue is the boys," he said, referring to his three adult sons. "What are they going to do? Have to be sure they have something meaningful to do for the next five years or so. Can't just cut them out. They love this business. We talked about it as a family. We agreed that staying in the business in order to enter the U.S. market would be a great opportunity for the boys. Can't see that issue addressed anywhere in the offer they made."

Truly, the issue wasn't money. Yet, viewed through a cultural prism, our client was behaving in a U.S. fashion, looking at issues in terms of money valuation only. Other cultures value relationships more. Though the Australian culture is very similar to ours in many ways, and they share with us the English language, one shouldn't underestimate the differences. Furthermore, the personal goals of the family-owned company had not been addressed or even considered. They were the issues that needed to be added into the valuation here. Three iron-clad employment agreements took care of that—and the deal was done.

All along the way, the U.S. company refused to do the Corporate Self-Analysis or to address the issues of the Culture Cluster. They thought they knew it all, but in fact they almost destroyed the acquisition opportunity.

II. The Financial Picture

The second step of the Corporate Self-Analysis is to get a clear financial picture of the organization. This is generally available and easily accessible. Part of the analysis, however, must look at the financial history and past plans of the company, examining in particular those areas in which financial projections were not attained and performance fell short of goals. The reason is not to point the finger at those who were responsible, but to analyze how plans have been implemented and what worked and what didn't for the company strategies. Clearly it would be foolish to make the same mistakes again.

The specificity of the analysis of the financial picture will depend once more on your corporate personality and desire for detail, but many organizations look at the past year or two, and especially, if appropriate, at the financial results of particular divisions of the company that may be involved in the planned alliances.

III. The Business Definition and SWOT (Strengths/ Weaknesses/Opportunities/Threats) Analysis

You have already developed a business definition in the creation of a domestic or global strategic plan. Now is the time to refresh that definition, updating it with your knowledge of the present status of the business in order to achieve two goals. The first is to define the existing business in the light of today's reality, and the second is to assess your future potential in the same light. The latter includes re-examining the estimates you've previously made about the behavior of your market, industry, and customer base and making a determination as to the regulatory climate.

This is also the time for a serious consideration of your corporate strengths and weaknesses. Some of them may have been touched upon in the Culture Cluster analysis, but any others that were not should be listed and discussed here. The logical consequence of this Strength and Weakness analysis will be the understanding of possible Opportunities and Threats (SWOT).

I like to simplify the information-gathering process and to use a technique that jogs the corporate memory when doing the SWOT analysis. The approach is to list the major characteristics of a company in a corporate profile on one page. The profile would contain categories similar to those in an annual report: a description of the company, its products and services, market, competition, and physical, human, and financial resources.

In this evaluation, it is important to outline both weak and strong areas. One company, for example, listed under human resources that they lacked organizational depth, a major concern in the development of alliances, since the CEO would be stretched thin in his ability to both run the ongoing concern and also develop strategic relationships that were Bet the Farm for the company.

Another company, having gone through the Culture Cluster and having realized that openness was important in the alliance development, added to their evaluation the fact that the company needed to raise capital. Although the family owners had thought that they were the only ones aware of that need, clearly everyone in the company already knew it. The listing of SWOT issues brought that issue into the open. The commitment of the employees increased, since they now felt as if they were on the same team as the family, and morale improved.

The purpose of this process is to place the decision to develop an alliance in context—to know what kind of organization you are, what you hope to be, and what the strengths are that will help you get there and to uncover weaknesses that need either to be eliminated or compensated for.

Product, Service, and Market Evaluation

Your SWOT information gathering should include a Product, Service, and Market evaluation. Ask and answer questions such as "Has the product been tested and proved in the home market?" Be aware that one of the first questions an international strategic partner will ask you is "How has the product/service been doing in the United States?" Be prepared with a thoughtful, well-researched answer.

The Impetuous Texans

A privately held company in Germany emerged as the potential partner for a mid-sized Texas company in the laser instrumentation business. The Texas company, also privately held, had been in business for ten years. They were active in the worldwide market as a leader in their particular area, which was a highly specialized medical field. During research and development into a laser-sensing system, they had discovered a new sensing device that they thought would have great appeal as a security device for the consumer market. They decided that the product should be sold first in Europe and then, once successful there, in the U.S. marketplace.

The problem for the Texas company was that they wanted to sell their invention in a market with which they were not familiar. An alliance seemed a natural solution. Looking for a partner, they discovered a German company with Europe-wide sales and distribution. It had a major presence in the security industry and was a market leader in Europe. The German company had hundreds of scientists who were experts in the security area and were working on new and im-proved versions of residential, industrial, and commercial se-curity sensing devices.

The partnership selection process had involved little plan-ning on the U.S. side. The company went immediately into the analysis of important markets and focused their attention on obtaining the broadest distribution network rather than on the appropriate alliance goals, strategies, and structure to achieve the desired results. Most of the company energy went into the identification of candidates and setting up introduc-tions and meetings.

Once they had decided to target a certain German com-pany as a potential partner, the U.S. company representatives traveled from Texas to Germany with a prototype of the product. The product was left there for the German company to examine, and the U.S. team returned home.

As you can imagine, the prototype was subjected to sub-stantial scrutiny. Sadly, it failed almost every test—it was heated, cooled, crunched, dropped, and shocked. The Texas company waited for a response. They did not hear from the German company for many weeks. Finally they faxed the company and received a reply, indicating that the product was not acceptable and that the German company declined the distribution opportunity.

What were the major failure factors in this alliance oppor-tunity?

1. The product launch was premature. Poor quality control and inadequate testing had made the product "an or-phan" in the parent company.
2. Cultural understanding was lacking on both the corpo-rate and country levels. The corporate personality of the U.S. company was the Hockeystick stage. The CEO was very enthusiastic and felt that his company's success in

the laser instrumentation area would naturally carry over into the consumer products business. The German company was Mature and rather patronizing. Although they admired the Texan company's success in the laser market, that was not their industry and so it had little real impact on them.

3. Overconfidence. The Hockeystick company ignored the possibility of a hostile technical evaluation. The U.S. company should have left their technical experts with the product in Germany in order to handle the evaluation and perhaps prevent the negative scrutiny that occurred. But the U.S. company had overestimated their product's readiness and ignored the advice of some of their more professional advisers, who had cautioned that the product should not be sent off without further testing and proof of viability—even test-marketing in the home market.

4. Too few resources, both human and capital, had been allocated to the project. The company was looking for a "quick kill" in terms of revenues from almost immediate distribution in the European market.

The result was loss of credibility as well as loss of time, bargaining power, and money. The Germany company also lost some time, but it was an inconsequential amount relative to their size and general research activities.

Some damage control was subsequently instituted. The CEO of the U.S. company visited Germany and recommenced discussions, promising a number of actions. First, U.S. technicians would accompany the product to Germany after it had been subjected to further R&D in the United States.

Second, the U.S. management would rework their long-term goals. They had gone backward into the process described in this chapter and realized they needed to gather information to understand their own Culture Cluster, Business Definition, Financial Picture, and SWOT analysis. This resulted in a new strategic direction for the company, which required that they rethink their strategic partnership strategy. The options analysis yielded an alternative that fit both their long-term goal to stay squarely in the medical industry and their short-term strategy of generating some non-labor-intensive cash flow.

They negotiated to sell the technology to the Germans, who saw a definite strategic fit between the valuable aspects of the U.S. technology and their already existing product base.

But had they pursued a more thoughtful process in the first place, both companies could have saved time and face while more effectively exploring the potential value to both in a relationship. In the end, the U.S. company sold the technology for far less than they had invested in developing it, and the German company, after further development, integrated it into one of their smaller product lines.

When you review the products and services of your own company, it is important to include market estimates and your company's percentage of market share, for both the past few years and the next two to three years, a time span that falls into the short-term category of operating strategy.

Organization Responsibility

Your SWOT analysis should include a process of pinpointing sources of strength for membership on the alliance team. When developing an alliance plan, a team approach is best. In the planning stages, the team should include representatives from the Corporate Planning Group and from Operations, and possibly the CEO. Cross-functionality is critical to broad-based responsibility for the alliance. That means that representatives from R&D, marketing, and possibly finance and operations should be included.

In in-company programs that have been attended by hundreds of employees from all levels of a company, I have often been impressed by members of, say, the purchasing or supplier management departments who have a great deal to contribute in the area of alliance implementation and also competitive intelligence gathering. However, such employees are rarely made part of an alliance-planning team, and they seldom get the respect they deserve. Their knowledge of some of the failure factors of ill-conceived and poorly planned alliances can be very helpful in this early analysis stage and especially in planning the implementation of the alliance.

Look out for the NIH ("Not Invented Here") syndrome at all stages of alliance planning, as well as NMH ("Not Manufactured Here") and other attitudes whose effect is to slow or prevent change or protect personal employee turf.

Human resources issues should also be discussed in the planning stage when the issue is addressed of who in the organization has responsibility for the alliance. I emphasize here again the Corporate Life Cycle and the various human resources that will tend to be used in connection with alliances in each stage of the cycle (see Figure 4-1).

A final point must be made concerning the human side of the capital investment associated with these relationships. In every alliance, no matter how low it is on the Pyramid of Alliances, the resource that must be available and allocated is "patient money." Investment returns from alliances are rarely immediate. Real alliance benefits result from patient and careful investment, so these financial investments should be accompanied by the human resources of talent, attention, and a realistic awareness of the costs. Thus although capital allocation is a function of the financial analysis of alliances and their returns, its effectiveness is influenced by the human element.

The alliance manager will often have the unenviable task of convincing senior management to develop reasonable expectations for returns from alliances. Especially in partnerships with

Start-up companies, there will be an ongoing problem with understaffing and undercapitalization. The alliance may be burdened with the Start-up's expectations for returns that are needed to keep the company in business. But returns can also be an issue with larger companies, which often have quite short budgetary cycles, putting them under constant pressure to meet short-term financial goals.

IV. The Possible Strategic Direction

After assembling all the information that is relevant, participants in this process will need to discuss the preferred strategic direction

Figure 4-1 Diagnostic: The Corporate Life Cycle and Human Resources Used in Alliances

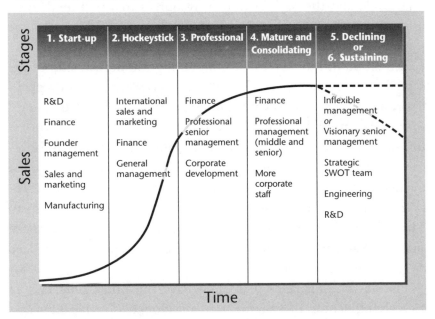

Stages	1. Start-up	2. Hockeystick	3. Professional	4. Mature and Consolidating	5. Declining or 6. Sustaining
Sales	R&D

Finance

Founder management

Sales and marketing

Manufacturing | International sales and marketing

Finance

General management | Finance

Professional senior management

Corporate development | Finance

Professional management (middle and senior)

More corporate staff | Inflexible management *or* Visionary senior management

Strategic SWOT team

Engineering

R&D |

© 1992 Larraine Segil

into which the company will direct its alliance activity. Utilize staff input if possible at all steps in this process of information gathering.

In many large companies, the strategic information gathering and the SWOT analysis is repeated by each division. This can be beneficial, but only if the information is shared and centralized. There should be a central repository for competitive analysis, such as in the departments of business development, corporate alliances, or strategic planning. Here consistent answers may be found to the questions posed in the course of the SWOT analysis.

In one company where centralized sharing of information and planning did not take place, a number of divisional managers found themselves bumping into their colleagues in the lobbies of the same potential partners! Or, even more embarrassing, a senior manager would find herself at a loss when the representative of a potential partner referred to his ongoing discussions with another manager in her company!

V. The Senior Executive's Input: "Golf Course" and "Designer" Alliances

If the chief executive has a preference for a particular type of alliance, this is the time to take note of it.

CEO input can sometimes manifest itself in a phenomenon that I like to call the Golf Course alliance. It arises when two chief executives meet on the golf course and agree that they "really should do something together." After all, they both run terrific organizations—wouldn't it be great to join forces somehow? Each CEO goes back to his staff and tells them, "Work on the problem. Let's do a strategic alliance with XYZ Corp."

Does this sound like an exaggeration? Plenty of chief executives will acknowledge—privately—that their early alliances were exactly of this nature. And representatives of corporate staffs are more forthright, vehemently confirming that this is how not only many of their past alliances evolved, but certain more recent ones, too.

The Golf Course alliance has a close cousin, the Designer alliance, which is a relationship that is announced with great fanfare and press coverage and hailed as a great new step toward changing an entire industry. The stock market analysts respond, while reporters write favorable articles in leading business publications on the potential effect the alliance might have on the market.

Then, strangely, it all fizzles and seems to disappear. Why? Usually because of inadequate strategic fit, and a short-circuiting of the process of strategic, corporate, and personality analysis. Those with the task of trying to make the much publicized relationship actually work will slow it down, finally burying it before any of the details can actually be worked out. The announcement of the alliance has the desired public relations effect, and then the media turn their attention elsewhere. The phenomenon resembles the latest high-fashion designs, which are given enormous press coverage, but few normal people actually wear such clothes, nor do they have real practical worth.

The telecommunications industry has fallen prey to this tendency and has announced a number of Designer alliances recently. The regional Bell operating companies, Sprint, MCI, and every multimedia company have been scrambling to enter diverse markets, and the resulting industry changes are threatening to blur the boundaries between telephone, entertainment, and retailing. But only time will tell whether many of the announced mergers and partnerships are simply Designer alliances—all fanfare, no substance.

Relationship Building over a Glass of Wine

Golf Course and Designer alliances should not be confused with an approach to alliances that I recently heard about from the chairman of a $1 billion technology company. When he and his German alliance partner, the CEO of a company substantially larger than his own, get together, their talk, he told me, is mainly about fine wine. The whole story goes like this:

The alliance had begun with a series of substantive conversations, the result of a strategic vision and teamwork at lower company levels that led to the decision to enter into a relationship between the two companies. A meeting of the CEOs was then arranged by both companies' teams. The deal was struck, and the alliance was established. Subsequently, the only time this CEO expected to discuss the alliance in any detail with his German counterpart would be if it were in serious trouble, facing problems that his management saw no hope of resolving—in short, if the relationship was in extremis.

Since that had never happened, the conversation when they spent the day together, about twice a year, was delightfully relaxing, accompanied by excellent food and wine. This kind of relationship building can provide the goodwill needed to resolve issues that may never come up, but if they do, will be critical to success or failure. Thus, even though the interaction between the CEOs may take place on the equivalent of a golf course, the planning and implementation of this alliance has been deliberate and strategic, not serendipitous.

VI. Selection of Alliance Strategy

You now have a lot of information about your company and, hopefully, about your potential partners. Now you need to decide what type of alliance strategy is most appropriate for you. Look again at Figure 1-1, the Pyramid of Alliances, on page 16.

Any structure in the alliance area will have an internal impact, no matter how low-risk you try to make it. But since you now understand how your organizational culture works, and the financial and strategic picture of your company, the risks can be managed. And that is what successful alliance implementation is all about.

Develop a Mission Statement

You should now be in a position to develop a mission statement for your alliance activity that has both qualitative (for example, "license 50 percent of new technology") and quantitative (such as "increase revenues by 30 percent") elements. An important aspect of the discipline of writing a mission statement is that it serves as a reference point to assess your company's success in the alliance. Success can be defined in a variety of ways. Further examples of statements of success expectations are ROI (return on investment), certain sales revenues from new products, expanded distribution, gaining entry into various world markets up to a certain percentage of penetration, and so on. Statements of goals that are too generic and undefined may lead to unreasonable and misaligned expectations after the alliance partners have entered into the relationship.

Success is a moving target, because as the industry changes and the partners' goals, personality characteristics, and life-cycle stages change, the goals and success criteria for the partnership will be affected. But some baseline of expectations must be developed at the outset of the alliance.

If you do not clearly state your success criteria in the planning stages, during the criteria-development and partner-selection stages as well as during pendency of the relationship, it will be difficult to make strategically correct decisions. If the availability of an attractive partner is driving your decision making, defining your success criteria at this point will assist you in looking clearly at the opportunity within your corporate guidelines, and will help you refocus your energies in a strategic direction.

Furthermore, memory is short. New team members in both planning and implementation may not remember the starting position in relationship development and may undervalue some of the concessions and compromises that have already been made, as well as the achievements already enjoyed. This is another good reason to develop a formal, explicit, written statement of your objectives and your success criteria for the alliance.

Summary

The Corporate Self-Analysis process consists of six steps, six areas of analysis:

I. The Culture Cluster
II. The Financial Picture
III. The Business Definition and SWOT (Strengths/Weaknesses/Opportunities/Threats) Analysis
IV. The Possible Strategic Direction
V. The Senior Executive Input
VI. Selection of Alliance Strategy

If the above six key steps toward successful partnership development have been taken, you will by now have come a long way toward avoiding common pitfalls in poorly planned and executed alliances. In this process, you have analyzed your business thoroughly and know its present status, since you have defined your strengths and weaknesses. Quantitative and qualitative objectives have been set, and you have clarified alliance responsibilities and developed an organization for partnership development. An outcome of the Corporate Self-Analysis may be that for reasons of corporate culture, market trends, organizational weakness, or financial considerations you decide that an alliance is not the right strategy for your company after all.

If you do decide to go forward and seek an alliance, you will need a timetable. Few alliances that are well thought through come together in less than six months, and most take a year; international alliances take even longer to develop, sometimes as long as two years.

Note that this is *after* the Corporate Self-Analysis process, which can be covered in not less than three months in large companies, usually longer. Smaller companies can generally accelerate the process to a couple of weeks. The good news about that part is that once done, there is no need to go through the process in detail again. All that needs to be done is to keep the culture elements up to date as the organization makes the transition into different life-cycle stages.

After the Corporate Self-Analysis the next major task is developing alliance partner criteria. That can take from a few weeks to several months, depending on the corporate personality. Declining companies may have rigid criteria that are a lot clearer than Start-up or Hockeystick organizations, which are changing so dramatically that their needs and worldview are moving targets.

Following closely on criteria development will be the partner search and evaluation process, negotiation, and closure. Then the real work begins: managing a changing and ongoing relationship for mutual success. These steps will be discussed in the next chapter.

5.
Preparing for
the Alliance

Some companies have no problem in finding alliance partners and are approached almost monthly with partnering opportunities. If you are one of those, your process for evaluation of a prospective partner can be greatly enhanced by using some of the methodologies in this book. Other companies have Golf Course alliance situations and must delicately and with some political awareness apply the Corporate Self-Analysis process described in the previous chapter in order to bring process and strategic justification to the alliance opportunity.

For many companies, however, the partner search is a tiresome and confusing undertaking. Especially for companies in the Start-up stage, obtaining the attention of the right executive of a potential partner, one with decision-making access or authority who will champion the project, can be time-consuming and frustrating.

Declining and Mature and Consolidating companies also have difficulties in evaluating projects that are Experimental or less (see Figure 2-5, "Project Personality Types" on p. 55). If your project falls into one of those categories, there may be delays in finding the right opportunity.

Any company having difficulty identifying the right partner candidates for a potential alliance will find the search and selection process outlined in this chapter helpful. Even those companies with partner candidates in view can benefit from the approach that is presented here, because it systemizes the process into a series of discrete steps.

Corporate Courtesy: A Matter of Strategy

Before approaching any potential partners you should give some thought to the question of corporate courtesy, which should permeate and underline every aspect of effective alliance development and management.

I have searched high and low for commonly accepted standards of corporate courtesy in U.S. culture and I have found that it is rare for people to be formally taught corporate courtesy. Good manners seem to be left to the personal upbringing of each individual. But how a company treats its employees, suppliers, and customers is a crucial part of its culture. Business courtesy is not only good common sense, it is also good alliance management strategy. That is why I mention the subject here.

The major elements of corporate courtesy are the following:

- Return calls promptly
- Write letters confirming appointments
- Say thank-you when appropriate
- Recognize extra effort
- Keep team members informed
- Ensure that support staff are pleasant, welcoming, and helpful both on the telephone and in person

In fact, you should treat a potential partner as a valued customer. Doing this from the start of the partner selection process will develop goodwill that may be crucial later on. A further reason for establishing a norm of courteous and pleasant behavior is that if a problem does occur, there is a strong likelihood that your displeasure will be noticed and responded to, since it will be in great contrast to your agreeable and helpful demeanor thus far.

Courteous business practices include sending a thank-you letter after obtaining financial and corporate information from a candidate or after a meeting. Keep logs of who called whom and whose responsibility it is to call back. When did you or someone else promise to return a call? Do it then or call to change the time or date. Reconfirm meetings. If changes have to be made, follow up with a note to thank the individual for accommodating your needs. Keep a candidate file but try to summarize incoming information so that a newcomer to your alliance team will be able to become familiar with the opportunity easily and quickly.

Note how the candidate was referred to your company. The person who made the reference will probably want to be kept informed on the progress of the relationship to the extent that confidentiality will permit.

These kinds of courtesies will distinguish you from your competitors in a small but memorable way. I have heard many CEOs complain about how difficult certain organizations were to do business with. One major industrial company executive recently commented in amazement on how a number of executives from a certain computer company never bothered to return his calls. His company had a technology that was breakthrough, industry-changing, of major importance, and they were looking for partners. The computer company's lack of courtesy in failing to call back meant they never learned of the opportunity and lost a chance that could have made a major strategic difference in their company's future.

The management guru Tom Peters has characterized courtesy in a customer service context as "delighting the customer." I suggest that you delight your potential partner. The relationship may not come to fruition, but they'll remember that your company was a delight to do business with. And especially if the potential partner is already a customer, supplier, or distributor, your company's reputation will be enhanced.

Let's now begin with the critical steps necessary for good alliance creation and management. There are fifteen steps in all.

Step 1: Developing Qualitative and Quantitative Partner Criteria

If you have followed the Corporate Self-Analysis process detailed in the previous chapter you should have by now created a mission statement for your potential alliance with goals stated both qualitatively and quantitatively.

The partner criteria can now be further clarified. Questions to ask yourself could include the following:

- What are the ideal characteristics of your alliance partner, in terms of size, market share, corporate personality, and position in the relevant industry?
- Could an existing partner (for example, a company with which you already have a distribution arrangement) be a candidate for an expanded relationship, perhaps one higher on the Pyramid of Alliances?

As a result of the options, goals, and objectives analyses you have done, your company now knows why it is entering into an alliance and what you hope to achieve. Now you can start filling in some details into the broad statements of earlier discussions. By the end of this partner-criteria exercise, you should have a list of criteria that are the ideal that you would be looking for in a partner. Some companies even give value scores or rankings to each of the criteria and prioritize them that way.

Step 2: Developing a Prospect List

Even if a potential partner has approached you, you may nevertheless want to search for a comparable partner while beginning the strategic fit analysis described below on the existing partner opportunity. As I have mentioned before, it is critical that partner analysis be proactive, not reactive. A partner that approaches your company, even if the opportunity looks interesting, may not be the optimum partner for the particular industry, product, service, or technology or may have an incompatible corporate personality. It behooves your organization to examine other partnering opportunities in the same area, if they exist, in order to verify that you are deciding to join with the best partner.

There are a number of sources to check out when you start to search for a partner to fit your criteria. You already know many firms with which you do business. They could be customers, suppliers, distributors, even competitors. All of them should be examined for potential partnering possibilities.

A commonly overlooked source of new partnering opportunities is the partners you already have. Extending a relationship with a known entity with which you already have a positive experience is sometimes an excellent solution to a partner search. On the other hand, you may not want to increase your dependency on that partner. Before undertaking any new extensions of the relationship, examine the strategic costs and benefits of doing so.

To find a partner candidate, some companies do large scans of the industry in which they are interested. They may use the help of organizations such as trade groups; if they are interested in a particular geographic area, they may approach local influencers, such as bankers, lawyers, accountants and tax advisers, consultants, bro-kers, and investment bankers for ideas and advice. Many formal studies on industry areas are completed by either trade groups or think tanks as well as consortia of large companies. Those studies could be helpful in identifying key and upcoming players in par-ticular industries. Other secondary sources are literature scans and data-base research, which can now be sophisticated, international, and broad in their scope.

Another source of information about emerging companies is in the venture-capital community. The particular areas of specialization by venture investors and the myriad of venture directories available can point you toward areas of new technology and research.

Visits to trade shows and conferences by either hired experts or your own employees will yield many opportunities that may then be more carefully researched.

Consular trade offices and U.S. government agencies such as the Department of Commerce can yield many leads for international introductions. A factor to be aware of, however, is that when you deal with unfamiliar cultures, understanding the status of the in-troducer of the company or the company itself—its in-crowd ver-sus out-crowd position in the country's commercial world—is much more important than just knowing the name of a company. The person within the potential partner company who champions the project in such a situation will also mean the difference be-tween success or failure. And since the courtship of international relationships is costly and time-consuming, it is critical to have the inside track early on in the game of partnership development.

Generally I do not do business in geographic areas where I do not have a trusted associate who is a country national. It takes years to cultivate such a relationship, but I've found it to be effort well spent. Many companies that operate internationally find that hir-ing locally will help shorten the time period it takes to become part of the "in-crowd," but the company may not easily or ever totally overcome this entry barrier.

Step 3: Strategic Fit Analysis

Once a potential partner has been identified, the next analytical step is to examine the strategic fit of the partner candidate with your company. There are many important questions to be asked at this stage. Some of them are:

- *Does the potential partner fit the quantitative and qualitative criteria you have developed?* Can you reach your return on investment (ROI)? Will their market share increase your market access?
- *Will the relationship meet the mission statement goals you have created?* The danger here is throwing aside your previous hard analytical work in the heat of the moment of finding an exciting partner opportunity. If you are going to change your strategy, realize what you are doing and make sure it is appropriate.
- *What are the details of the partner's business, such as their management capabilities and the intention of key managers or project champions to remain in the partner company?* I was once involved in the acquisition of a company, where my associates and I made the classic mistake of not investigating closely enough the capabilities of the managers who were key to the acquisition. We found that, after a fairly short period of time, the most important manager left, and the less important ones stayed and had to be terminated.
- *What do you know about the key champion in the partner company— the individual who will carry the flag of this alliance within her own company?* In an alliance that falls on a low level on the Pyramid of Alliances (see page 16)—say, a distribution agreement—the key champion is especially important, since the project will languish if no influential individual is constantly striving to push it up to a higher level of project importance.
- *Have you diligently collected information on the company—its business history, financial background, and general position in the industry (vis-à-vis market share or technology prowess, depending on the*

type of alliance)? Gather information that is publicly available, such as Dun & Bradstreet reports (which, it must be remembered, include information supplied by management) and SEC filings, and analysts' reviews. Other data may be necessary, depending on the type of alliance; much of it, such as marketing-, technology-, and product-related data, will be available from the company.

- *What is the strategic potential for your company of a partnership with this candidate?* Be sure the strategic direction of the partnership is consistent with your Corporate Self-Analysis, covered in Chapter 4.

- *Is there another partner in the same industry that would be a better candidate?* Note that if you were in reactive mode—merely responding to other companies' approaches—you might not be able to answer this question!

- *In this relationship, what would the risk exposure for your company be in terms of both embedded and migratory knowledge transfer?* The answer to this question could save you a great deal of money and an unpleasant partnership dissention.

Jordan D. Lewis of the Wharton School at the University of Pennsylvania distinguishes between two types of information:[1]

- *Migratory knowledge* is *what* a company communicates.
- *Embedded knowledge* is *how* a company communicates.★

Look at what is normally negotiated in an alliance—technology value, capital investment, number of products sold, license fees, the numbers that can be crunched in a variety of ways to transfer value, creating an outcome that can be equated with "success" and "mutuality." It's generally all in the contract, and it is migratory knowledge—*what* a company communicates, information—that is overtly and deliberately being moved across company boundaries. (Lewis's *Partnerships for Profit: Structuring and Managing Strategic Al-*

★ These issues are handled in my course "Strategic Alliances." See page 239 for details.

liances [The Free Press, 1990] was one of the first books on alliances and is still a good resource.)

What about the way you talk to your customers, how you reward your employees, the process you use to analyze your competitors, the layout of your production facility? This is also valuable know-how possessed by the company. But are these areas touched on in the contract? Generally not. Are they valued in monetary terms, and when awareness and knowledge of them are transferred is value paid for? Rarely. This is embedded knowledge, and in some instances it may be so important as to constitute the core competency of the company.

One large computer company realized that they were transferring embedded knowledge in their partnership with a high-flying organization in a high-growth stage. Their partner was learning their core competency: the way they service their customers. But that had not been bargained for in the deal-making process, and its unwitting transfer was making the sales and service people who were implementing the relationship very uncomfortable. And so it should. It was their market advantage, what had drawn their partner to them in the first place.

What do you do if you are in a relationship and realize that you are transferring the life's blood of your organization without intending to? Conduct a quick and efficient relationship audit and then undertake a reconfiguration, placing parameters around the relationship, effectively cordoning off the areas of unintended transfer. It's not easy and may ruffle some feathers. The partner may cry foul and see a diminution of the trust relationship that was developing. If the opportunity was not negotiated for, though, this may be an important moment to restate the intended goals of the partnership. It may also present an opportunity for a renegotiation. In either case, the reconfiguration will still be preferable to the loss of competitive position by one of the partners three years hence.

- *What is the partnering activity of the candidate company at present?* If they are a good partner in other relationships, the likelihood is that they will do well with your company, unless there are significant personality clashes on the corporate, individual managerial, or project level. Conversely, if they are a difficult and uncompromising partner with others, it is likely they will behave the same way with your company. By this point in your corporate self-education, you no doubt realize that corporate culture is very difficult to change. In the presence of a compelling business consideration, even if a partner personality is troubling, you may nevertheless decide to go forward. Knowing a potential partner's foibles before entering a relationship can make the difference between success and failure. Hence the importance of using the Mindshift method of personality diagnostics, now augmented by real-life experience of the company's activities in another partnership. Gathering that information may not be difficult. If the candidate company is in the same industry, your network of contacts will tell you what you need to know. If it is in another industry, advisers such as industry experts and consultants will be helpful.

- *What if there is a poor strategic fit between your firm and the potential partner?* If the partner candidate is not a good fit, do not discard the information you've gathered about them. As you continue to evaluate partner candidates, you may find that your criteria change as the reality of the marketplace changes your ideal criteria to those that are feasible. Thus, a rejected partner may become attractive at a later stage of your evaluation process.

Step 4: Ranking the Strategic Fit of Your Candidates

Develop as much information as possible on the candidates prior to establishing contact in order to put yourself in a strong position for negotiations later on.

As mentioned briefly earlier, many companies rank their candidates according to how they meet the strategic criteria that were previously developed by your alliance team. Each criterion is given a value, then the values are combined to get the ranking. The list of candidates is then ranked. If the alliance-planning team has to make recommendations, this kind of organization of the material can be very helpful.

Summarize the technology or product and market review, all the information and data that has been gathered, and evaluate the strategic fit of each candidate with your company, the appropriateness of each candidate as a partner for your organization, in keeping with the goals and objectives that you have analyzed and developed during this process.

The companies with a good strategic fit will go on your primary candidate list ranked in order of priority as their characteristics fit your goals. Place the other candidates on a secondary candidate list. These too can be ranked.

Now begin relationship development with the companies on the priority list. Proceed going through the entire list of candidates regardless of a favorable outcome on any of those first contacted. If several positive responses result, you are in an excellent position to negotiate with the most desirable candidate. The ranking and contacting processes are interrelated and iterative. As contacts are made and information is gathered, especially in Step 5, when meeting and evaluating candidates, ranking developed in Step 4 may change. Using this process will help bring discipline to a process that for many companies is an opportunistic approach that allows excellent candidates to be missed.

Step 5: Meeting and Evaluating Candidates

During this process of early relationship development, the initial contact should ideally be made by people with a previous personal relationship with the candidates. For primary candidates where no personal relationship exists, a member of the alliance–planning team should be assigned the responsibility of making initial contact.

Who should be contacted? In small companies, the top executive; in large companies, the vice president or officer in charge of new product development, corporate business development, new relationship development, corporate opportunity, or strategic alliances.

Gather as much information as possible prior to, during, and immediately after the first meeting regarding the current status of the business, financial overview, marketing overview, product-development overview, and any joint ventures, licensing agreements, or strategic partnerships presently in place. The purpose of this proactive and energetic approach is to verify the information you have already received and adapt and improve understanding of the appropriateness of the partner for your stated goals. The partner candidate will appreciate your efficiency, interest, and alacrity. You, on the other hand, will not waste time with partners that do not strategically fit your needs. Continue exploring and investigating any existing relationships they may have in order to understand their modus operandi in partnerships.

Positioning your company in the other company's eyes is important. Do not send out the same package of information to every candidate. Prepare a series of packages "selling" the opportunity to each particular candidate and tailor the packages to each company. Information in a typical package for a marketing alliance will include general company background such as annual reports, SEC filings, and other related publicly available documents, as well as all product-marketing materials, advertising brochures, examples of warranties, etc.

The first meeting is attended only by those in the alliance team who are considered critical to the creation of a first impression— for example, the vice president of marketing, along with the director of alliances or business development in a marketing alliance. The goal is to convince the prospective candidate that there is mutual benefit to be derived from a strategic relationship, so focus on the mutuality element, namely, what's in it for them and how the two companies together could leverage an opportunity better than if attempting to do so alone. The candidate will be impressed by your knowledge of his business and by the thoroughness of your preparation.

If the partnership is a marketing or distribution opportunity, gather details on their marketing programs and sales volume. Tailor your questions to the criteria you have established to be vital and mandatory for your strategic partner. This can be done both during and after the meeting.

If the proposed arrangement is a co-marketing agreement, understand their existing advertising and sales promotion programs; their marketing strategy; how they deal with price issues, warranties, and sales policy; their sales-incentive program, if they have one; the organization of the sales department; the customer-relations function, and so on. Obtain from the candidate a random list of customers with whom you can check out the company's reputation—or, if you are uncomfortable asking the candidate for this list, get one from other external advisers such as industry consultants.

If the proposed arrangement is a research and development project, find out the qualifications and background experience of the key scientist(s) who will be working in the joint venture. Ask also how the R&D department maintains documentation security. This often is a point of great disagreement: A number of companies consider their partners to be sloppy in procedure and process. Certainly companies in different stages of the corporate life cycle will see the need for these security measures in different lights.

Another area for concern is the other company's existing procedures and practices concerning changes in engineering information. Are the candidate's engineering personnel active in presenting papers at seminars and industry meetings? If so, be sure your arrangement spells out the permissibility of such presentations and when they are and are not appropriate.

Compare the candidate's technology development with that of the competition in order to establish whether they are in fact the right strategic joint research partner.

After the first meeting, the team member who has been appointed the liaison with that partner opportunity should write a thank-you letter. After every meeting this person should develop a meeting memo that goes on file. This enables new and existing members of the alliance team to keep track of activity easily, so that follow-up can be carried out more efficiently.

Step 6: Getting to Know the Corporate Champion

It is important to get to know the individual or team who will become the champion of this opportunity within the candidate's company. Developing an ongoing relationship with those managers preempts any "turf" issues or "Not Invented Here" problems that may arise in the future.

As you learn more about your partner candidate, work on developing mutual trust and commitment to the opportunity. It is healthy to recognize equal though differing needs for the relationship. The forging of personal trust relationships at this stage may be the key factor later, when the honeymoon phase of the partnership is over and turf issues as well as changing perceptions cause rifts in the partnership relationship.

During the process of gathering all the information that will enable you to evaluate the strategic fit of the candidate with your organization and its goals, meetings will continue, and the gradual sifting of deal points will begin. Discussions will gradually narrow after strategic fit appears valid, and the lead representatives of each company will exchange viewpoints on the various issues relating to the specifics of the alliance such as each partner's definition of success, the answer to WIIFM (What's in it for me?), the proposed duration of the alliance, its goals and limitations, who will be involved in managing the relationship operationally, and so on. In fact, each partner is now easing into the negotiation stage of alliance development and the end result should be both a building of trust as well as the narrowing of focus on to the items that need final negotiation.

I recommend placing potential deal-breaking or divisive issues on the table at this stage. The way your partner candidate handles compromise, dissension, decision making, and managerial personality will become evident during this process, and that knowledge may not only assist you in making a final decision but will also help you later in the management of the relationship.

Step 7: Looking Out for Land Mines

Besides the information gathering just described, your legal and accounting team should also be involved in researching the implications of your alliance. I suggest you also examine such eventualities as the possibilities of a "green" lawsuit, a hazard in the biotechnology arena as well as in advanced materials. When I acquired the small advanced materials distributor mentioned earlier, I discovered some rather nasty toxic products in the inventory that became my responsibility to dispose of. What was even nastier was that I learned that liability for such a product followed the owner personally to her grave, regardless of whether that particular owner retains ownership rights in the company.

Be aware that a majority of the members of the European Parliament are currently supporters of the Green (environmentally aware) political persuasion. The company with which you may be developing an alliance may have some environmental issues to face. You do not want to become embroiled in their battles.

Another land mine, one for your accountants to sniff out, is the so-called eighty-twenty syndrome: 20 percent of a partner's customers may give them 80 percent of their business. Unless you are aware of this, you could be vulnerable in a relationship where that partner loses a major customer, and with it half or more of its revenues.

Step 8: Obtaining Internal Approval

Covering yourself at your own company and obtaining clear approval from the CEO and top advisory staff is a critical element in managing this phase of the alliance-development process. If reliable internal approvals are not obtained, a decision maker may emerge later on in the process and pull the rug out from under the relationship. Besides the potential loss of a good business opportunity, and a rather embarrassing career moment, this may also be seen by the potential partner as an inability by your company to be trusted or an unwillingness to commit. It also doesn't bode well for the company's industry reputation.

This internal approval political problem is often exacerbated with companies in the Declining and Mature and Consolidating stages. Politician managers generally try to avoid making decisions (less activity means more approval and no risk) and Farmers are rather complacent, so that decision making takes a long time. As an Old Boy network member, the Farmer has to check with lots of people before he feels absolutely comfortable in going forward. A company like this may gain a reputation in their industry for never being able to develop partnerships. Every decision must be internally approved by so many decision makers that someone is invariably left out, causing most partnerships to grind to a halt in the negotiation stages.

Step 9: Creating an Implementation Plan

Alliances conceived entirely by the planning and corporate departments without the active participation of the operations managers who will ultimately have responsibility for the project are doomed to failure. There are many examples of a well-executed business opportunity and strategic fit analysis, which is followed by faulty implementation.

A failure point occurs when the alliance-planning team hands off the project to the alliance-implementation team. One way to avoid this is to create the implementation team by adding a few more members to the already existing group. Some companies prefer to have an entirely separate team working on the implementation scenario. Whatever your choice, this is the moment when the alliance-planning team must translate their excitement, knowledge, desire for the benefits, and awareness of the costs of the alliance to those whose careers may depend on the alliance's outcome.

Companies that close the deal, sign the contracts, and only then bring in the managers who will manage the relationship will encounter problems with management acceptance of the relationship goals and risks. On the other hand, if operating managers are involved in at least the later stages of the candidate selection and deal-negotiating process, they will be informed and knowledgeable about the candidates that have been ranked high in the evaluation analysis. They will be prepared to start working on the alliance-implementation plan.

Step 10: If Partner Development Lags, Try a Quick Fix

Sometimes the partnership-development process begins to slow down or lag. Industry changes may cause one partner's attention to be distracted and the level of project importance may start moving from Market Extending to Experimental or worse. This may be the time for a "quick fix" solution.

Pilot Program as Quick Fix

A Mature and Consolidating company wanted to enter a new industry and had selected as a partner candidate a company in the Hockeystick stage. After early steps had been taken to develop the partner relationship, momentum started to diminish. The champion in the Mature and Consolidating company was losing heart, feeling as if he were "pushing a huge boulder up a glass mountain" as he tried to keep the alliance process moving forward within his own company. The partner company was eager to move forward but the Mature and Consolidating company was risk-averse and political.

The solution was to create a pilot program with the partner candidate, using a simple business combination low on the Pyramid of Alliances. This was a short-term move that was consistent with the long-term goals of both companies. The solution could not involve new, unproven technology, since the risks were too high that the pilot program would not achieve its goal: to prove to the decision makers in both companies that the project was worth continuing. The pilot program had to be able to show that the relationship fit the strategic criteria of the Mature and Consolidating company in order to ensure that the project did not slide beyond Experimental into the nether regions of totally unimportant projects.

The Mature company was also having difficulty understanding the fragmented and complex nature of the target market, which was in the health-care industry, and in integrating the perceived opportunities into their own corporate culture. The pilot program offered an opportunity for these issues to be explored. It would also give high visibility to the business opportunity within both companies, and possibly identify a market entry point.

The Hockeystick company, on the other hand, was experiencing its own problems. Their need for speedy decisions, focused on action not process, meant that their level of frustration with the Mature company was so high that they were at the point of walking away from the opportunity. However, they would also take with them their increased awareness of the business opportunity concept that had been jointly discussed with the Mature company. Thus, the Hockeystick company could possibly walk straight into the arms of a willing competitor. This fact was well known to the Mature company's corporate champion and it helped drive him to find the "quick fix" solution.

If partnership development flags, a critical question needs to be asked and answered: Are the symptoms of lagging enthusiasm indicative of a fundamental inability of one of the companies to function effectively in the relationship? If so, are there cultural issues too complex to be overcome? If the answer to these questions appears to be no, a small-scale pilot project may be a useful testing ground for a full-scale alliance later on.

In defining the pilot program implementation steps, the parties must determine what they consider to be "success" for the pilot, clearly a more limited goal than for the whole relationship but consistent with the strategic intentions of both partners. It is important to include a valuation discussion regarding your subsequent relationship with the same potential partner in the design of the pilot program. Otherwise, you will not only educate them but will increase the value of their company in your disfavor, should you have to negotiate with them later. Their company post-pilot has an increased value as a result of your joint activities and your company's contribution to their know-how.

Step 11: Applying the Mindshift Method to the Partner Selected

The purpose of applying the Mindshift method is to understand how rapidly your company will respond to changes in the environment, a business downturn, or competitive forces as well as how the culture and relationship fit will work with your company, your managers, and the project in contrast to theirs. You need to ask and answer the six questions explained in "Applying the Mindshift Method" in Chapter 2 (see pages 57–59) with reference to your partner's life-cycle stage, its corporate personality, the managerial personalities of the partner's key managers, and the Project Personality Type of the alliance. Then consider the fit between what you know about your company, your managers, and the project's role in your company strategy and the analysis you have made of your partner. Is there a good fit? Is there relative compatibility? No partnership is perfect. Can you live with the differences? My research shows that the differences increase over time, and eventually (within three to five years) personality differences are more important than business justification and lead to a perception of alliance failure.

The research also shows that power struggles by managers lead to alliance failure. The managerial personalities most likely to be in conflict and thus cause a perception of alliance failure are Warriors and Politicians. Hunters and Farmers are most likely to be compatible (see Figures 2-2 and 2-3, pages 30 and 39). The pairs of Corporate Personalities most often in conflict are Hockeystick with Mature and Consolidating, Hockeystick with Declining, and even Hockeystick with Sustaining. Hockeystick and Professional corporate personalities are quite compatible. The most compatible corporate personalities are Professional with Mature and Consolidating. As you would expect, the closer the partners are in their life-cycle stages, the better they can relate to and understand each other.

With respect to Project Personality Type, the chances of alliance success are higher when projects are Bet the Farm for one partner and Market Extending for the other. Even when a project is Experimental for one partner but Bet the Farm for the other, its chances of success are better than if the project is Experimental for both partners. It is always a wise strategy to increase the project priority for all alliance partners.

Step 12: Final Predeal Evaluation of All Relevant Information

All the information you've gathered should be assembled prior to the final step of having your attorneys draft an agreement. The question must be asked one more time: Does the opportunity meet your objectives? Some time will have passed since the initial contact with the candidate, and the fortunes of their operations may have changed. Managers may have come and gone, the industry could have changed, and, most important, the processes you have gone through will have uncovered a variety of personality traits— corporate, individual managerial, and project—that may increase risks and decrease the chances for success. You may decide to modify your original ranking of the company to a lower one.

Balance the human dimension with the business issues. If either one is unappealing, the candidate should be rejected. One strategic alliance manager of a utility who had developed twenty-seven alliances once told me, "When I am developing an alliance, after a number of meetings with the folks from the candidate partner company, if I get the feeling in my gut that the personal relationship is going to encounter difficulties, I pull the plug on the deal. And whenever I don't, and permit myself to be swayed by the business opportunity, I live to rue the day. It never works unless both business and personal considerations are acceptable." The 235 companies that were surveyed after applying the Mindshift method agreed. In fact 73 percent of the companies surveyed felt that corporate personality was most of the time a contributing factor to failure, 63 percent attributed failure to managerial personality, and 58 percent to project personality. As can be seen from the percentages, most of the companies surveyed felt all three categories were important factors contributing to failure.

Step 13: Managing Any Predeal Glitches

Include all the stakeholders in the final stages of relationship development. This is the time to look out for unexpected issues to arise. If someone appears at this moment who doesn't favor the deal, he or she may ultimately destroy it. Such a person is likely to be one of the internal politicians who should have been consulted in the internal approval step and wasn't. It could be a board member, who could destroy the deal by influencing other board members to vote against the alliance if it needs board approval.

Turf issues may now arise as middle management who will be involved in the alliance suddenly feel job insecurity. These people have to be brought into the trust-building and alliance-development process in order to develop their support or to position them in a nonthreatening role to the alliance. If in fact their jobs are at risk from the alliance, there is little that can be done to assuage their concerns. The damage that they can do to internal morale must be controlled either by repositioning them in the company or terminating them as soon as possible—for example, in a case where the decision had already been made to terminate them because the alliance was providing an outsourcing opportunity for the company in a cost-cutting mode.

Another glitch that often occurs is in the advent of legalese in the formal deal structure (we'll look at the role of lawyers in Step 16). Agreement documents normally contain reams of boilerplate and federal regulatory verbiage and this may be quite disturbing, even to fairly sophisticated international corporate executives. Such agreements will even intimidate small company CEOs in the United States and often annoy non-U.S. companies large and small. I recommend that you send legal agreements into a foreign culture accompanied by a cultural interpreter, someone familiar with the cultural ways of the other national and corporate culture who can hand-deliver the multipage document. In fact, it's a good idea in an international alliance to have a cultural interpreter with business expertise present throughout the whole alliance-planning process to smooth over these and other cultural miscommunications.

An Invisible Decision Maker Surfaces

One kind of last-minute glitch that is especially prevalent in venture-backed companies is the arrival of the "invisible decision maker." Situations exist where the entire management team of a Start-up company is involved in partnership development but where the real power lies with the investors.

In one such case, a venture-backed Start-up company in the laser field had determined that a European alliance would be essential for their growth into the Hockeystick stage. They were already selling in Japan and the United States. After a very successful trip to Europe, where they met with a number of companies interested in their products, they received two distribution-relationship offers. However, the venture investors now saw dollar signs instead of a growth opportunity. After consulting with investment bankers who did some financial projections, the investors came up with an outrageously high valuation for the company. They halted further funding for the company, effectively hampering its immediate growth, and sent out a prospectus asking for a buyer. After six months of futile bickering, the company fell apart. The CEO and all the senior management left, the European companies who had made the original distribution offers were nowhere to be found, and the venture investors folded the company into another one, the valuation having sunk to the cost of assumption of liabilities.

In this case, the invisible decision maker was one of the venture capitalists—not the lead one but an investor whose driving considerations were his portfolio devaluation, not the well-being of this particular investment. Ostensibly authority lay with the chairman, the lead investor, and the management team, but this was not the real source of authority, which lay with the secondary investor, who gathered board support and predominated. The failure to obtain his internal approval in the beginning was a critical flaw in the alliance-development process.

Step 14: Negotiating the Deal

Negotiation is a skill that is used all day in general management activity. In alliances negotiating skills are even more indispensable, for the very reason that alliances are continuing, changing sets of relationships that require constant redefinition of activities and responsibilities, and teamwork.

Individual managerial personality has a lot to do with your choice of negotiation style—a style that feels comfortable and will work best with your partner. Whatever negotiation style you choose, you should combine it with the Mindshift personality diagnostics. They will give you an edge.

Negotiation styles that work well in U.S. businesses may be totally ineffective in other countries. The work of Stephen Weiss and William Stripp at New York University[1] is very helpful in establishing guidelines for international business negotiations. Weiss and Stripp maintain that in every negotiation with persons from other countries there are twelve variables that have an impact on the outcome of the negotiation, either positively or negatively. Understanding these variables can assist you in presenting your side of the negotiation and also in interpreting and understanding the negotiating team that is sent to work with your company. Using these understandings combined with the other factors mentioned in this book, you may be able to move the project personality from Experimental to a higher level, or vice versa. The following discussion of the aspects of cross-cultural communication that are pertinent to the alliance-development process are those that evolve in negotiation both before and during an alliance.

American negotiation style generally consists of offer and counteroffer until consensus is reached. An alternate approach is based on problem solving, which I see often in the joint-venture process between aerospace companies, and again in research and development partnerships, where collaborative problem solving is acceptable to the corporate culture.

A further model is the process of debate and persuasion. U.S. executives will always anticipate rebuttals to various offers and have a backup position on key issues. This style may not be acceptable in other cultures. It requires comfort with confrontation and a belief that each partner is entitled to convince the other of the rightness of his decision.

In alliances, the best approach is problem solving, as it is the only methodology for reaching compromise. Offer, counteroffer, debate, and persuasion may be useful at certain points, but the end result to target is an equitable solution that maintains the always elusive goal of mutuality. This approach also offers the possibility of creating a third alternative, something better and different from what either party had previously considered as an option.

It is important to adapt your business and negotiation styles to be compatible with the culture in which you are functioning. It is a cultural trait of the United States that we tend to oversell; in the United Kingdom, understatement works far better. Toning down the "sales" approach to negotiation will be less jarring when you are working with U.K. executives. In China, the arguments of persuasion may include macro issues, such as what we consider legitimate costs of doing business—an issue that arose with one Chinese official recently. An American executive was becoming increasingly irritated by the number of people from the Chinese side who appeared to take part in the negotiations, especially before mealtimes. Of course they then joined the group for the meal, which was paid for by the visiting American. When she commented grumpily that she was getting tired of all the extras, the official said quietly to her, "Here in China, it is of concern to us who will fill the rice bowls of our people." It took the executive some research with her cultural interpreters, friends in the Chinese community, to discover that what the official meant was that this—and all the other personal demands for housing, food, even training—was part of doing business in China. The executive added these items to her cost of doing business, and in the contract she eventually obtained she was more than adequately compensated for her effort.

A caveat must be added here. In all circumstances remember that your stereotypical expectation may be wrong. Judge the corporate and personal characteristics of your counterpart in the context of her culture. She may be the exception, not the rule.

The team members and their personalities are key to the course of the negotiation. Your company is sending a nonverbal but powerful message in your choice of alliance team members. The status of the participants will affect the outcome of the discussions. Someone with too high a status may intimidate and embarrass in non-U.S. cultures, since the partner will fear that they will insult you by not having the same-status managers present; conversely, a person with too low a status or one from the "out-group" could cause insult. Someone who is well respected, trusted, and from the right in-group may be able to create trust in the most difficult of circumstances because of his or her personal attributes. Especially in emerging economies, where the legal enforcement mechanisms are not well developed, such individuals may be valuable because their word of honor and promises can be depended on.*

The Illusion of Authority

Sometimes the perception of authority is different from the reality. This occurs in domestic as well as international al-

---

* These issues are handled in my course "Merging Globally." See page 236 for further information.

liance development activities. One executive, the CEO and owner of a $200 million company, recently recounted how in his negotiation with a $5 billion company he was assured innumerable times that the person he was negotiating with was the decision maker. However, he doubted this. After six meetings over a period of four months, about halfway through the seventh meeting, the "decision maker" pushed his chair back from the table and said, "I do believe that this has to be taken above my head. We had better table this discussion until it can be taken to higher authority."

The executive finally met with the board of directors and they approved the project. The process, instead of being irritating to him, was a wonderful learning experience. He said that after the first two meetings, he realized that his counterpart did not actually have the power to make decisions. It became a kind of game. He started taking bets with his chief financial officer to see how long it would take before the potential partner's representative would take him to the real decision makers.

The team members must also pay attention to protocol, which in some countries is a critical value. Bypassing the chain of command in a hierarchical society can kill a project swiftly.

Whether your partner is part of a culture that favors the group above the individual or is more inclined to favor the individual over the group will affect your choice of team leader and the reliability of your evaluation of your partner's team leader. Is he interested in personal glory or primarily in the good of the organization and the community? Assessing these possibly contradictory goals will assist you in understanding the motivations of the partner leader. Ego can be a tremendous incentive for those in autocratic cultures, where power sits at the top of a hierarchy; playing to that ego of the man at the top can be a good strategy. Ego can also be a major deal breaker in individualistic cultures, where it can cause the NIH (not invented here) issue to arise, especially where an individual manager sees that his career is threatened.

Warrior and Adventurer managers are especially prone to undertake ego-driven actions. One Warrior manager recently described himself to me as a "loose cannon" and remarked that he reveled in that perception of his behavior. He noted that he won many battles through mere audacity, asking for contract items that he was told many times by advisers would never be agreed to by the other parties, or wouldn't pass SEC muster, which he obtained by being deliberately obnoxious.

In other cultures this behavior may be unappreciated and, especially where relationship building is the focus, may destroy any possibilities of a partnership. In the United States it may be an asset. Understanding these critical differences may help you to recognize what is going on and develop counterstrategies.

The Exploding CEO

In a CEO roundtable conference called the World Technology Executives Network the companies represented hailed from the United States, Europe, and Asia. One of the American CEOs, who ran a missile manufacturer, was a Warrior manager of extreme characteristics. He had a humorous presentation style: He would seem to explode with energy, raising his voice and yelling almost directly in someone's face to make his point.

In one of the discussions that took place, he apparently assailed another American CEO, an Adventurer born in China but raised in the United States who ran a multinational computer company, using his normal, frighteningly energetic approach. The Adventurer had a reserved manner. The Warrior yelled that the Adventurer was doing an incredible job running his company, and that he should stop whining about what he hadn't done and admire what he had!

The two men had met before, and the computer company executive handled the Warrior manager's outburst with patronizing and amused tolerance. The twenty-five other international executives present at the roundtable, however, were appalled. I had prepared the participants individually prior to the meeting, traveling to their headquarters throughout the world. At that time I mentioned that I had seen occasions when tempers and opinions became vociferous and pointed, having on a number of occasions facilitated CEO groups that included Warrior and Adventurer managers, who abounded in the technology fields.

But nothing I said could have prepared the non-U.S. executives for the outburst that they heard. The other American participants thoroughly enjoyed the confrontation, which ended in the two executives' becoming good friends—amazing behavior to those from other cultures.

Warrior managers would do well to heed cultural differences in negotiating styles. Confrontational behavior, both verbal and non-verbal, can be very insulting in other cultures and is not considered amusing, entertaining, or a sign of strength as is sometimes the case in the United States.

Coming to an agreement can be a tricky issue. In Western cultures we determine that the written word, signed and attested to properly, is the main evidence of an agreement. In some other cultures, massive transfers of goods and money may take place without any formal agreement, just letters of credit and bank transactions, bills of lading, and shipping and transfer documents.

You may have someone's word and thereby their agreement long before any documents are signed. More difficult for Westerners to handle is that you may have a signed agreement, properly attested to, and then negotiations seem to go on post-contract and the deal terms seem to be constantly changing. In some cultures it is felt that the agreement is no more than the beginning of the negotiation. Once you understand what is happening and adjust accordingly—it's not easy; I know because I've struggled with this myself—you will be better able to continue to position yourself to your organization's advantage.

One executive who was well experienced in alliances once told me, "Alliance creation and alliance management are one and the same thing. You will start off negotiating, and end up doing the same thing."

I agree and I take it one step further. An alliance that is not re-negotiated after a number of years may become irrelevant or unworkable. Negotiating strategies are important skills for alliance managers and implementers.

A final point to remember is that in privately held businesses, the key negotiator may be the CEO, who may also be the sole owner of the business and may speak personally on behalf of his company-child. He will be sensitive to the negotiation in a way different from officers of a public company. The latter may be more concerned about what you will do for them than what you will do for the stockholders.

Step 15: Managing the Legal Process

The lawyer's perspective can either destroy a perfectly good relationship or greatly improve the understanding of the issues at stake. Being a competent alliance lawyer is an art. I have met a number of in-house attorneys who are highly competent and sensitive to the relationship and trust issues that are an integral part of the partnership arrangement. The same can not always be said of outside counsel.

There are a number of different approaches to the relationship of in-house counsel to the operating managers. Some managers insist on having legal counsel in on the alliance-planning sessions so that the lawyers are aware of the issues discussed and resolved in that stage. Although many managers, especially Warrior managers, do not want their in-house counsel present at preliminary alliance discussions, I believe that counsel must be included in the Corporate Self-analysis process in order to understand the way the organization makes decisions and all the other elements described in detail earlier. Managers that recognize the value of educating in-house counsel in this way will generally want counsel to be involved in the early stages of candidate evaluation and information gathering, so that they will also be familiar with ranking issues, compromise points, and the reasons why specific choices have been made along the line.

The picture changes, however, once the partner enters the picture and meetings are held to start building mutual trust. At this point, having legal counsel in the room may give the wrong impression, that is, that the meeting is a negotiation rather than a trust-building session. Although some managers ask legal counsel to be present but to say nothing, the fact is that the mere presence of a lawyer or legal adviser in the meeting room may have a chilling effect on relationship development. It depends on the cultures, both corporate and country, of each partner.

There are different points of view on the role of legal counsel. Some managers insist that lawyers should have absolutely no personal presence in the alliance-development process, but they keep them informed with meeting memos as the relationship develops.

The stage of the company in the life cycle may also lead to variations in lawyer-dependency behavior. Small and entrepreneurial companies, generally Start-ups or Hockeysticks, will balk at bringing their lawyers to meetings because of the high cost of doing so. Some smaller companies have told me that they could barely afford the legal fees required to review and negotiate the 150-page legal contract sent to them by a Declining company partner.

Outside counsel pose another problem. Most commercial-transaction lawyers consider themselves competent to review and draft alliance agreements. Not all of them actually are, however.

Transaction lawyers may not understand the intricacies of relation-ship development that far transcend the written word. I hope that some of them read this book. So much trust can be undone by ask-ing for too much, demanding that actions be taken that could price the alliance out of reach of a smaller company, or that run counter to terms that were reached through a painstaking process involving months of relationship development and compromise.

I recommend that parties to an alliance create a simple memoran-dum of terms, in everyday nonlegalese, that have been agreed to and compromised upon. That document must be the foundation upon which the legal agreement is drafted. Clauses that need to be in-serted for liability, federal or state regulations, or other reasons should be personally explained to the other partner, so that they do not feel their trust has been breached. The entire contract-drafting process has to be carefully managed with consideration for the increased cost of fees that large firms working for Mature or Declining companies can impose on Start-up firms, which may be represented by a single small law firm.

Another aspect of the legal process is the time it may add to the implementation schedule. Again, good interpersonal communica-tion between the corporate champions and their teams will assist in resolving misunderstandings.

From a technical point of view, the legal art of structuring cor-porate strategic partner arrangements could involve these related tasks:

1. *Nondisclosure agreements* Agreements to keep confidential in-formation that is designated as confidential by either party
2. *Evaluation agreements* Agreements giving one party the abil-ity to examine the other party's information or products for the purpose of evaluating strategic fit for a defined period of time, with the added requirement of confidentiality
3. *Letters of intent* Specific expressions of intent to do business together in a defined arena

These will precede the development of the contractual elements that will eventually be incorporated into an alliance agreement.

One feature of an alliance agreement should be the alliance's long-term working mechanisms: a plan for how conflict will be resolved. This should not be through the usual mediation, arbitration, or litigation options, but rather by means of positive methods to keep a fundamentally good relationship together. Such methods might include being able to refer a problem to various higher levels of management in order to ensure the participants will receive assistance in resolving their difficulties. Termination of the alliance is not always the best solution, especially regarding alliances where embedded information has been transferred on the way an organization does business and its corporate culture. The relationship of embedded knowledge and country culture is discussed in detail in Chapter 6.

Where partnerships are meant to be short term, exit strategies should be clearly set forth in the agreement. Some alliances could succeed as short-term relationships but are mischaracterized as long term. These often die a miserable death as a consequence of the growing misalignment of goals.

An alliance can also be structured as short term with the intent of tiptoeing into the relationship, perhaps on a lower level of the Pyramid of Alliances, and leaving open the opportunity for the relationship to migrate up the Pyramid into a longer-term relationship. One example is when distribution agreements are entered into and later the companies merge. What must be attended to in the agreement in this instance is the possibility that early in the relationship an unfairly low valuation is placed on the company being acquired. The "acquiree's" desire for a higher valuation must be balanced against the acquirer's desire not to pay a premium for a company that is now worth more as a result of their joint activities. A skillful attorney will address this issue delicately.

The assistance of legal counsel who are sensitive to the trust issues, who are educated as to the realistic goals and cultures of the parties, and who are trained to look for compromise and conflict resolution rather than confrontation and termination will be very valuable for companies at every stage of their life cycle. Such people are truly contributing members of the alliance-planning team.

So far we have covered all you must know to be prepared to have the very best chance at implementing and managing an alliance well. Many of the mistakes made in managing an alliance have their origin in the lack of preparation to do so. If you prepare well, constantly modify plans and behavior, and take into account the Mindshift approach and macro issues, your potential for managing the alliance effectively is greatly enhanced.

One skill set, however, is so important that it deserves its own chapter, and that is managing cross-cultural alliances. These are among the most challenging of alliance relationships and present interesting opportunities for astute managers with facilitative and collaborative skills to show their excellence. In Chapter 6 we take a look at that fascinating world.

6.
Cross-Cultural Alliances*

A senior executive in a Declining company in the defense electronics industry who was nearing retirement once cornered me after a conference at which I'd made an impassioned presentation on the importance—and difficulties—of communicating across cultures. He had very limited international experience, but in his market niche had managed to do rather well in the United States.

"Trying to do business in foreign countries with local hires is like teaching a dog to climb a tree," he said. "I suppose you could do it, but it's so much easier to hire a squirrel." I laughed. He didn't; he was serious. I sighed. In some cases, like this one, you can't teach an old dog new tricks, especially if he is a Politician in a Declining company.

If you are over thirty-five, you may have progressed in your career thus far without a taste of doing business in another country. But the young executives who are nipping at your heels are very

*A detailed handling of cross-cultural issues is in my course "Managing Globally." See pages 239–40.

likely people who have spent a year or two in another culture or speak a second language. They will be well equipped to understand the dynamics of a business situation when non-U.S. cultures are involved, and their know-how may make the difference between success or failure in a competitive or collaborative situation. However, if you haven't lived in another culture, all is not lost. You can still learn to communicate across cultural lines. It takes awareness and some level of commitment, but it can be greatly rewarding.

In cross-cultural situations the processes of alliance building and the Mindshift principles remain valid, but the managers who are selected should be trained to become expert not only in intercorporate communications, feedback, and problem solving, but also in the extra complications caused by cultural dissimilarities.

The first part of this chapter will address specific cultural mistakes that many companies have made and that you can avoid. The second part will relate the Mindshift system to the results of a thirty-country survey of macro-cultural management practices done by the European Management Forum Foundation,[1] a respected research group based in Geneva. Throughout the chapter you will find examples of specific cross-cultural opportunities where some companies have gained great competitive advantages from their cross-cultural learning.

Experience Helps—Sometimes

Sometimes cross-cultural joint ventures can reap enormous benefits, especially for companies that are experienced in doing them. One such company is Corning.

Success and Failure at Corning

Corning has formed more than fifty joint ventures, many of them international, in the past seventy-three years, and as self-reported by their management and according to their success criteria, only nine of them have failed, well below the average 55 percent figure cited by Professor Kathryn Rudie Harrigan of Columbia University's Strategy Research Center.[2]

One of Corning's alliances was with the Korean manufacturer Samsung. The Corning-Samsung venture allowed Corning to enter the Korean market with a large local manufacturer of consumer electronics, including television sets and tubes. Corning had invented the all-glass television tube and was a major supplier worldwide but needed better access to Asian markets. Samsung wanted to move into television manufacturing. Both parties believed that the time frame for a successful alliance should be ten to twenty years. Mutuality existed, and the cultural differences were manageable, since both parties respected and appreciated what the other company had to offer. Corning recognized and valued Samsung's knowledge of the market, sales expertise, distribution techniques, and manufacturing capability. Samsung valued the technology and supplier experience that Corning had developed over the years.

When the new joint venture, Samsung Corning, was created, it had three potential customers in Korea—Samsung, Goldstar, and Daewoo (originally Orion). Corning spent time visiting Goldstar and Orion before the alliance was created to learn how to win orders from them. This was also very helpful in their future understanding of their joint-venture partner. The venture was managed by the Koreans from its inception, and was important as a source of product and service to Samsung. The focus of all management was on developing customers for the venture, not just providing opportunities for Samsung. It has been considered by both parties to be a success, and now has revenues of over $500 million.

However, another joint venture of Corning's did not do so well. This was the Corning joint venture with the Vitro

Group in Mexico, a large glass manufacturer that concentrates on drinkware. Although Corning was not in that line of business they did consider that Vitro's lines would complement their consumer business. They created a binational venture in which Corning owed 51 percent of the American operation and Vitro owed 51 percent of the Mexican operation, and ran the operations as one company. The structure did not work, however, because the two companies had misaligned expectations and could not overcome their cultural differences.

What both companies really wanted was distribution. The risks, capital investment, and human resources committed to the project were all excessive in light of the modest objectives the companies really shared. There was no need for a full-blown joint venture.

The human resource area is where most of the potential cross-cultural problems reside and in this case actually were encountered. Another structure could have been selected, one that would lessen the issues of control as well as the need to work together as intimately as is required in a joint venture. This would be one that was lower on the Pyramid of Alliances in terms of risk, use of human resources, and capital—namely a distribution deal.

The companies ultimately came to the same conclusion. After reexamining their goals and the realities of their chosen structure, the joint-venture parties reconfigured the relationship and developed distribution agreements for each other's products in their respective home territories.[3]

An example of a successful intercultural collaboration on a grand scale that could have been an abysmal failure but actually ended up a colossal success is the four-nation Airbus project. The partners were Britain, Spain, West Germany, and France, and each group had its responsibilities well defined, with mutually negotiated milestones for each team to achieve. The management of the project was decentralized so that decision making was on the local level. This short-circuited lengthy debates and possibilities for misunderstandings.

Dropping tariff barriers in the European Community does not mean that there is now a "Europerson," a homogeneous European personality spanning the European Community. National cultural differences are as strong as ever. However, despite the great differences in style, philosophy, and language among the Airbus team members, collaboration and a desire to do a job well overcame the intercultural issues that could at many points have torn the project asunder. Unlike Americans, Europeans generally are used to working closely with people from other cultures, and here the country differences became issues the team members were determined to overcome, since the venture was one of great strategic and economic importance to all concerned. Airbus's powerful position in the worldwide aircraft market is evidence of the success of the venture.

Another variable that must be taken into account by those looking to develop cross-cultural alliances is the fact that there are subcultures within many country cultures. Consequently, it is important to verify whether the cultural assumptions that you are making are valid for the specifics of your alliance issues, or whether they have been modified by particular subcultural characteristics.

For example, the degree of formality is an element of a country's culture, but in the United States it differs greatly among subcultures. Acceptable dress in southern California, where the relaxed style is preferred, may be unacceptable in Chicago or New York—unless you are talent in the entertainment industry, where the rules are that there *are* no dress rules. Indeed, not all subcultures are geographical. In insurance and banking, suits are the general dress code no matter where you are geographically. Regional, ethnic, religious, and industry subcultures are just a few of the many sets of rules that make up the diversity of the United States.

Similar regional differences exist in other parts of the world too. The residents of Beijing consider themselves to have different values than those who live in southern China, many of whom are considered opportunists by Beijingers. The Shanghai elite have a view of life different than either of the other two groups. And there is no such thing as a "China market." Taiwan, southern China, and Hong Kong may seem geographically close when viewed from North American shores, but their cultures are vastly different.

Be especially aware of the pitfalls of making generalizations in cultures that value individualism, since the spectrum of individual behaviors will be vast and varied. In cultures where the group is more important than the individual, broad statements as to cultural preferences are a little less hazardous.

Other specific differences in country cultures will not be addressed here, since it is a topic that requires its own book. The point of this chapter is to make you aware that differences exist, can be understood, and, in the best circumstances, can be planned for in an effective management approach. Executives must learn personal cultural self-awareness and understand how to integrate corporate culture and country culture into management systems that can work in both American and non-U.S. environments. This includes the design of project-management skills in a culture where time is viewed differently, developing incentives in a culture where group approbation is more important than money, and so on.

Cross-Cultural Learning Exchanges

A benefit that is often undervalued in cross-cultural alliances is the transfer of techniques that work in a non-U.S.-based alliance back to this country's operations. Sometimes U.S. companies presume that they will always be in the position of teacher and the international partner in the position of learner. Major opportunities are lost by taking this attitude. Senior management often expresses a desire for two-way learning, but workers who are on the front lines of operation can see successful practices in foreign operations of the same company as a threat to their job security.

Motorola Management in Malaysia

Motorola's plant in Penang, Malaysia, is regarded as the best in productivity, quality, and innovation in the company's Land Mobile Division. It has an all-Malaysian, two-hundred-member research and development team of engineers who help to develop next-generation two-way radios and cordless phones.

Their quality-control program relies in part on thousands of recommendations from employees. More than 41,000 suggestions were received in 1993, some of which resulted in more than $2 million in savings. Every part of the production process was examined, with suggestions ranging from minor to substantial. From interviews with employees of the venture, it appeared that the individuals who gave their input were motivated by the feeling of belonging to an important endeavor, of being a family of workers who would all benefit from productivity and process improvement. They thought in terms of the good of the group rather than the gain of one individual.

This approach to quality has become a key part of Motorola's blueprint for developing a well-trained, motivated, and highly productive workforce in Malaysia, China, and Vietnam. However, although these training and motivational programs have been successful in Malaysia, they have not met with wholehearted success in the United States. Perhaps the reason is expressed in an old Asian proverb: The swallow that imitates the salmon will drown in the stream. To be effective, management techniques must be acculturated. Once you understand the differences between a culture that values the group above the individual (Malaysia) and one that values the individual and his or her personal rewards above all (the United States), the need for modification becomes clear.

In Malaysia some successful approaches were the creation of a group incentive (rather than incentives tailored for individuals) and of a sense of family among the workers. These approaches were not successful in the United States when adopted in the same form as used in Penang. The approach had to be modified for the U.S. culture. American workers required more than praise and group accolades. Some plants have instituted cash rewards as incentives for individuals.

A common issue for workers in both areas, however, is the fear of losing their jobs. After management made it clear that they desired the U.S. group to develop a team approach and to modify a cultural preference for individual gain, workers in the United States were moved to go along with the idea of contributing substantive suggestions (some early ones were as mundane as moving the trash cans) and developing a feeling of group responsibility. The Malaysian approach ultimately reaped benefits in the United States—but only after cultural norms had been taken into account.

In a global economy with shifting labor markets, no one can rest on their laurels.[4] Work migrates to wherever quality, cost, and efficiency can be managed so as to derive a better return on capital and time invested. Just as Malaysian enterprises represent competition for U.S. plants, so Chinese industry is competition for Malaysian operations. Shanghai is fast becoming an international engineering center, competing with Taiwan and Singapore. Bulgaria is emerging as a hotbed of computer scientists. Even the Malaysian workers will eventually have to recognize that there are other regions of the world where work can be contracted for at a lower cost. The list of examples is long and still growing. South Korea is becoming influential worldwide in the areas of memory chips, and Bangalore in India as a leading center for software development. Cross-cultural competition for labor and technology is a reality that is impacting every company that does business internationally, and cross-cultural alliances must adapt as well.

The Cross-Cultural Interpreter

Many organizations underestimate the extra effort and time that cross-cultural alliances take. One effective tool for managing the unique challenges of such alliances is the cross-cultural interpreter. By that I do not mean a language interpreter, but rather someone who either comes from or has lived at length in both your and the partner's cultures and will understand the nuances of verbal and nonverbal communication and perception in both cultures.

Remember that in some cultures it is of critical importance whether the people involved come from an in-group or an out-group. A cultural interpreter who comes from the in-group and possesses the right family, educational background, and connections can make a substantial difference in a culture where relationships and status are more important than contract terms. You may want to use either a locally hired employee, one from within your existing organization whose functional skills are less important than his or her ability to bridge both cultures, or an outside consultant with the same skills.

Understanding Value Across Cultures

It is difficult for an organization to compete in the global arena without international partners and alliances on various levels of the pyramid. This is so not only because of the need to defray immense fixed costs, but also in order to truly understand cultural perceptions of value.

Since 1988 Texas Instruments (TI) has initiated memory-chip projects with Hitachi and Kobe Steel in Japan, Acer in Taiwan, and Canon and Hewlett Packard in Singapore. Not only do these alliances shelter TI from cyclical slumps in the U.S. dynamic random access memory (DRAM) market but in the upswings they also generate cash that TI uses to diversity into higher-margin products, such as digital signal processors.[5] Developing alliances has enabled the company to defray their capital investments rather than doing it all themselves, and to increase the value of those investments by using its cash to leverage their technology.

Riding the Political Waves: Honeywell in Russia

Honeywell, Inc., has a twenty-year presence in Russia, having had an office in Moscow since 1974, through the Cold War, Gorbachev, *perestroika,* and *glasnost.*

The company used its understanding of the culture and the political uncertainties of the region to select the right partner from a political perspective. Honeywell first took an equity position of 49 percent in a joint venture with the Ministry of Mineral Fertilizer in 1988. They increased their equity control to 50 percent in 1990 as their partner metamorphosed into the State Agrochemical Association of Russia. In 1994, they bought out one of the other partners in the venture and now have a 70 percent interest in the joint venture.

The management team that oversaw the venture included Belgians, Austrians, and Germans, who initially assisted the Russians to get the alliance up and running. Thereafter 100 percent of the team were Russians, some of whom had been on assignment in the Honeywell U.S.A. operations and others who had been trained at the company's western European sites. Honeywell aggressively integrated corporate personalities and cultures with the country's cultural and political realities. And they placed a time limit on the strategic alliance arrangements. Value was given to both the tangible position they held in the Soviet joint venture, and their ability to learn from the participants in the venture, the realities and opportunities of doing business in that region.

Mike Bonsignore, the chairman and CEO of Honeywell, said in an interview for the James W. Mckee Forum on International Management in 1994, "We keep analyzing how convergent the strategies are and the pressures the enterprise may be under five years out as opposed to what it looked like when we put the strategic alliance together. That gives us the necessary escape hatch if we have to use it."

He also affirmed the need for the right customer and the right partner: "That is absolutely paramount in these high-risk markets where the chances of failure are already above average."[6]

The strategy of selecting the right partner, from both a political and a business point of view, is also important in developed countries, where chances of failure are exacerbated because of cultural miscommunications. Bruce Torp, the technical director for Tel-Comm Products Division, a major division of 3M Corporation, has commented:

> When Japanese and U.S. companies negotiate, mutual incomprehension often results because the amount of profit that is acceptable over a short time span in Japan is lower than the amount that is acceptable in the United States. . . . 3M's subsidiary in Japan employs a few Americans and mostly Japanese. Most Americans are on five-year assignments. The United States must move people to Japan, not just [let them] sit here [in the United States].[7]

Many large Japanese companies struggle with the same issues. However, even smaller companies with limited capital recognize that staying in the protected and interrelated environment of their home territory is not the way to compete for the future in a global economy.

Japanese Executives Only, Please!

The chairman of a $700 million Japanese telecommunications hardware maker noted recently that alliances may be the only way for his company to expand overseas. "You can't live in your own world anymore. . . . Finding the right partner re-

gardless of nationality is the key to future global success."[8]
His company was considering an offer to enter a wireless-
communications joint venture with a French conglomerate.

Only 277 out of 10,000 employees of the Japanese company work in Japan. Nevertheless, the company makes all
strategic decisions at the home office in Japan. Japanese executives run all foreign subsidiaries and most key decisions are
made at headquarters. This structure could end up causing
the company to become uncompetitive. This company will
need to reexamine its business processes in order to decide
whether its understanding of partnering in a global economy
will also mean transferring decision making to foreigners and
rewarding them accordingly.

Unless they do, they may not obtain the best local input,
access, or skill. They will continue to have a Japanese perspective, which like any particular cultural focus could hamper
them when they compete with companies that have a global
perspective and successfully "transculturalize" their organizations and strategies.

Sony is a company that has moved further than almost any other
in the direction of true globalism. Sony's American and European
operations have until recently been run by an American and a European, who also sat on the board of the parent company. Recent
management changes at Sony have removed Michael Schulhof, a
senior American executive, and it remains to be seen whether Sony
will continue its open-minded approach of the past. Headquarters
still has the major role in decision making, non-Japanese executives
have been given more responsibility than at other Japanese companies, and Sony has been an attractive place for foreigners to work.
English-speaking skills are highly valued at Sony. "We hire and pro-
mote people mainly for their ability to do business," says Tamotsu
Iba, Sony's executive deputy president and chief planner, "but if you
can't speak English here, you can't fully do your job."[9]

The Nomads of Texas Instruments

Some companies have developed a special team of managers to investigate, create, and implement international activities. Texas Instruments has a group of more than two hundred professionals—dubbed The Nomads—who have set up chip-fabrication plants in Italy, Taiwan, Japan, and Singapore since 1990.

This shows an admirable efficiency in that the same team repeats similar activities in a variety of countries. However, when these teams leave, experienced managers with cross-cultural expertise must be in place. As Richard M. Ferry, president of the executive search company Korn/Ferry International, says, "Having a well-stamped passport isn't enough to make an executive a global player."[10]

Such global functionally focused teams are not unlike the teams that might be employed by a Visionary manager moving a Declining company into Sustaining. She will typically bring with her a team of experienced professional managers with whom she has worked in the past, and will also use some key individuals in the Declining company who show drive and promise (if there are any left—many innovative managers leave companies if they linger in Decline) as she attacks areas in the organization that need a new approach. As with the Nomads of TI, the team's mandate is to work quickly, efficiently, and aggressively. The most effective teams incorporate operating managers who can be relied on to continue the work once started, and will have already bought into the concepts and strategies of change, since they were involved from the beginning of the team change effort.

The important lesson to extract from the above examples is that intelligent alliances that are cross-cultural will take into account a definition of value that includes defraying their investment over various countries, with a series of alliances, maybe even using targeted teams with special expertise to set up the relationships, but leaving talented culturally aware managers in place to manage the ongoing alliances. This can have the result of leveraging capital and labor investments worldwide.

Four Elements of Country Culture

Seminal work on pinpointing the characteristics of a country's culture has been done by Dr. Geert Hofstede, whose book on the subject is called *Culture's Consequences.* He has isolated and defined the following significant elements:

1. *Power distance:* "The extent to which a culture accepts that power in organizations and institutions is distributed unequally."
2. *Uncertainty avoidance:* "The extent to which a society feels threatened by uncertain or ambiguous situations."
3. *Individualism/Collectivism:* Individualism is "a loosely knit social framework in a society in which people are supposed to take care of themselves and of their immediate families only. Collectivism is a tight social framework in which people distinguish between in-groups and out-groups; they expect their in-group (relatives, clan, organizations) to look after them and in exchange for that owe absolute loyalty to it."
4. *Masculinity/Femininity:* Masculinity is "the extent to which the dominant values in society are assertiveness, money, and things, not caring for others, quality of life, and people."

Hofstede ranks forty countries according to how these national culture concepts are manifested.

The United States ranked twenty-fifth on the Power Distance dimension; that is, Americans are relatively unwilling to accept power differences among groups or individuals on the basis of inherited or unchanging characteristics (class, caste, etc). This explains our general openness toward opportunity for advancement on the basis of performance, not family or in-group contacts (although there are good arguments that certain subcultures within the United States have less opportunity for advancement than others and that other subcultures rely heavily on in-group contacts.

The United States ranked thirty-first on the Uncertainty Avoidance characteristic. This means that we are a society that is not threatened by ambiguous situations.

The United States ranked first on Individualism, highest of all the forty countries surveyed, and twelfth on Masculinity, which was above the mean on the scale of forty.

The usefulness of Hofstede's analyses as a tool is clear when one imagines an American manager in a foreign environment, attempting to manage without an educated awareness of the different cultural issues that surround every decision.[11] The American manager's response may vary from continuing, ever-increasing levels of discomfort to complete dysfunctionality.

When the Mindshift personality diagnostics are superimposed upon Hofstede's analyses for the purpose of addressing problems in an intercultural alliance, we find a kaleidoscope of issues. What is the corporate, individual managerial, and project personality of the alliance partner? What are the differences between the partners with regard to the four Hofstede criteria? How will the ongoing alliance-management problems be affected by these variables? These are important issues for the managers involved to address.

Cultural Differences—The European Management Forum Survey

In 1987, a respected research group based in Geneva then called the European Management Forum Foundation (now IMD) in its

Annual Report on International Competitiveness published a summary of their worldwide survey of nearly two thousand managers. They examined differences in these managers' national cultures.[12] The figures in this chapter show some of their results.

1. Motivating the Workforce

Figure 6-1 illustrates the results when the following two questions were asked of the two thousand managers:

1. *How great is the sense of drive, responsibility, and entrepreneurship among managers of your nationality?*
2. *How willing to identify with corporate objectives and priorities are the workers of your nationality?*

The responses to the first question are shown vertically as the estimate of talent of the nation's management. Highest ranking were the United States, Hong Kong, Sweden, Japan, Thailand, and West Germany.

The responses to the second question, shown horizontally, placed Japan far ahead of all other countries, with Taiwan second and South Korea third. The United States was twentieth out of twenty-nine countries, and Australia and Greece were last.

How should we interpret this data?

The United States is a culture that greatly emphasizes the value of individualism above the interests of the group. It is therefore logical that its management culture will evidence a constant balancing of corporate cultural identification with the interests of the individual. A corporate culture that is consistent with the conflicting belief systems of the group versus the individual requires flexibility and can work very successfully.

Apple Computer is a company whose culture balances the interests of individual, often highly eccentric technologists with corporate well-being. The company has created a streamlined career track for technologists who do not wish to assume managerial responsibilities and prefer to focus specifically on technology development.[13]

Figure 6-1: Cross-Cultural Comparison of Management's Talent for Motivating the Workforce

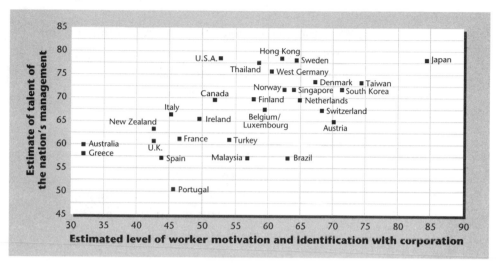

Source: European Management Forum Foundation Survey, 1987

This advancement track enables them to achieve promotion, identify with the company, work individually or in teams, and reach the level on the hierarchy of needs that the psychologist Abraham H. Maslow considered to be the highest, self-actualization. Maslow's hierarchy ranks the need of individuals, which range from survival (food, water, air, and light) to needs of a sophisticated level of human development: the fulfillment of personal dreams and hopes, both intellectual and emotional, after the material necessities have been secured. According to Maslow, the fulfillment of survival needs is a prerequisite for fulfillment of "higher" needs.

Other companies in the United States have developed equally individual-oriented cultures while creating a strong worker identification with the corporation. Many of them, like Apple Computer, are in the high-tech field, where individual contributions are greatly valued as a part of corporate culture.

Applying the country characteristics to the Mindshift system, and particularly to the six stages of the corporate life cycle described earlier, presents some interesting challenges. For example, Brazil is an emerging economy with great potential, although inflation concerns still abound; it is striving to become one of the economic stars of Latin America in the twenty-first century. According to the EMF survey, the level of motivation of workers in Brazil and their sense of identification with the corporation falls somewhere near the middle of the countries surveyed (see Figure 6-1).

However, management talent available in Brazil to motivate those workers was in the lower third of countries surveyed, while the United States, Hong Kong, and Sweden were the highest and had more managers available to motivate workers.

Now place this in the context of a Declining company that needs a Visionary manager for its survival. Such a person is far more likely to appear on the scene in Hong Kong, the United States, or Sweden, where management talent is available to motivate the labor force, than in Brazil. Thus, a management team developing cross-border alliances has to take into account national management characteristics of the dominant culture, the life cycle of the organization with which you are thinking of partnering, and relevant corporate personality characteristics—as well as the business justifications for the alliance.

Of course, your alliance may include managers who do *not* fit the norm of the dominant culture as reflected in the EMF survey but are part of a subculture or are individual renegade managers. A $3 billion software company's recent cross-cultural alliance in Japan included a Japanese manager who was as entrepreneurial as any American manager could be. In addition he hired only senior managers who, like him, were renegades. Making cultural assumptions regarding this group would have been a grave mistake, since they clearly belonged to a small subculture that resembled American cultural characteristics more closely than Japanese.

Managers can only motivate workers who want to learn and strive to improve. Therefore if one adds the other EMF dimension of level of worker motivation this means that workers in Sweden (very high on the scale in Figure 6-1) will be more likely to go along with the plan in order to preserve their place with the company and to become part of the new Visionary manager's approach than workers in other countries.

The EMF survey found that workers in the United States fell into the lower half of the graph for worker motivation and identification with the company and so among the countries surveyed would be among the least willing to accept change and strive for improvement. One interpretation may be that the individualistic nature of our culture is more likely to cause workers to question authority and change, looking for a customized approach as a solution rather than a group-dominated vision. Depending on the culture, this could either be seen as a weakness or a virtue.

Note that a limitation of the EMF survey may be the fact that they examined manager-worker relations as evidenced by management-union relationships. The United States did not fare very well in that area, owing possibly to the relative powerlessness of unions in the United States compared to other Western countries.

2. Delegating Authority

The EMF Foundation Survey looked at the willingness of managers to delegate authority. This willingness indicates that a manager has sufficient interaction with and confidence in a subordinate to delegate part of his responsibilities to that individual, trusting in the subordinate's skill and judgment in the implementation of a given task. It does not mean escaping from responsibility for those tasks. The results are shown in Figure 6-2. Japan scores highest, Sweden next, and the United States third, with Spain and Greece at the bottom of that scale. Canada places 16 out of 30 countries surveyed.*

---

* The top-scoring countries (other than Japan) have flatter hierarchies. Japan is seen by some to be less hierarchical, and by others, more. A more subtle interpretation would be to see Japan as a culture that delegates but where power as a cultural element is dispersed by the process of group consensus, leading to hierarchies of groups rather than individuals.

Figure 6-2: Cross-Cultural Comparison of Managers' Willingness to Delegate Authority

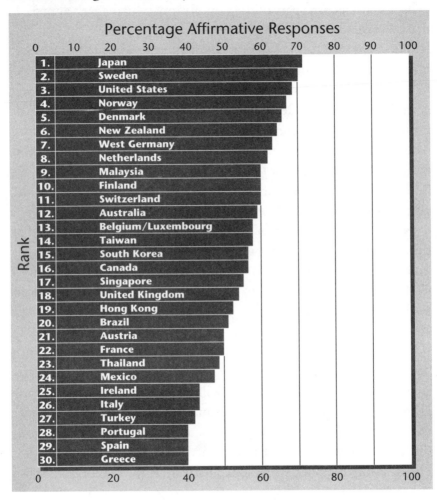

Source: European Management Forum Foundation Survey, 1987

Relating this national characteristic to the life-cycle phase of the organization, one of the outstanding characteristics of the Adventurer manager in the Start-up company is his need for control coupled with a lack of willingness to delegate. I call it noncontinuous delegation, since the Adventurer has a short fuse and often will start to delegate a task, only to retrieve it for himself, impatient because he feels that he can do it better and faster. This makes a Start-up fragile in its management structure and lacking in management depth. Developing an alliance will be a challenge for the Adventurer, since it will add significantly to his already overfull workload, which tends to reflect reactive crisis management. Combining these traits with the EMF survey: Even though generally U.S. managers are willing to delegate, if they are the Adventurer type, their personalities will often override their cultural tendencies.

In countries such as Greece and Spain, where according to the survey the national culture teaches a lack of willingness to delegate, the ability of an Adventurer manager to come to terms with his own desire for control and the need to empower his subordinates will be exacerbated by his national cultural tendencies.

3. Marketing Push and Product Quality

Figure 6-3 compares the reputations of selected countries in the area of marketing push and product quality. The questions asked were related to the abilities of managers to sell product and how this "fresh" ability related to the quality of the product sold. The EMF survey found that the countries with the highest reputation for both market push and high-quality products were Japan, Switzerland, Sweden, and Denmark, in that order.

Although the United States was second in marketing push to Japan, we were fourteenth in reputation for product quality. This implies that the marketing and sales presentation of U.S. companies is not consistent with the promised product quality. In 1987, when the survey was taken, the reputation of U.S. companies was relatively tarnished when product-quality reputation was evaluated. It was found that those who push the product too hard run the risk of losing credibility, not just for themselves, but for the business in general, especially if the quality of the product sold is not as good as is represented.

The Mindshift approach can identify the personalities of companies that might suffer from the characteristic of overmarketing and underperforming. Start-up companies often show this charac-

Figure 6-3: Cross-Cultural Comparison of Reputation for Marketing Push and Product Quality

Source: European Management Forum Foundation Survey, 1987

teristic. Their unrealistic expectations can lead to lack of product readiness or poor market testing. Mature and Consolidating companies and certainly those in Decline err on the other extreme: They test and retest the product to such an extent that the market window closes; product quality may be there, but the market has slipped away either to a competitor or a new and more innovative product. In either event, the perception in international activities at the time of the survey was that some United States companies promise more than they deliver.

4. Willingness to Create and Exploit Technological Innovation
Another area explored by the EMF survey was the relationship between the stated readiness of corporations to exploit innovation and the average number of patents granted per 100,000 inhabitants of the country (Figure 6-4).

Figure 6-4: Cross-Cultural Comparison of Technology, Creativity, and Corporate Willingness to Exploit Innovation

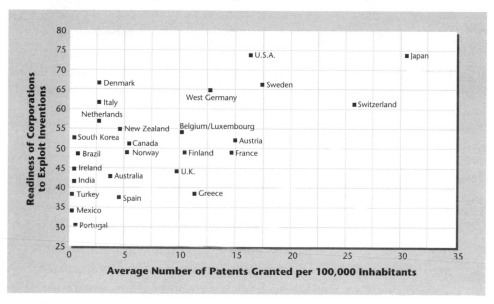

Source: European Management Forum Foundation Survey, 1987

The Japanese scored by far the highest in number of patents—double the number of the United States. Furthermore, and contrary to common belief, the two thousand managers surveyed felt that Japanese corporations exhibited the same level of willingness as U.S. companies to exploit those innovations.

The survey underlines the danger of national complacence and stereotypical perceptions. The United States has been perceived worldwide as the most innovative culture and the most embracing of novel ideas and technologies. This survey dispels that impression and shows that Japan is a world leader in technological innovation.

The danger of stereotypes is also seen when the Mindshift approach is applied to the perception of innovation. The generalization is that innovation thrives more readily in individualistic and entrepreneurial companies, especially those in the Start-up life-cycle stage with Adventurer managers. Yet many Japanese companies that are

filing large numbers of patents and whose activities in new technological development are prolific, are Mature and Consolidating.
Their willingness to exploit such innovation is often backed by deep
pockets filled with capital, low-interest government subsidies, and a
national policy that supports that segment of industrial research.
These stakeholders should not be underestimated in their powerful
global reach. In the area of technological innovation personality
characteristics must be interrelated with national cultural norms.

Planning the Cross-Cultural Alliance

Developing a plan for a cross-cultural alliance should follow the
process and methodology explained in this book, with one important difference: The key skill of managers involved in building such
alliances must be the ability to work in ambiguous, unfamiliar,
cross-functional, and transcultural relationships.

The team must include a cultural interpreter—someone with
experience, contacts, and respect in the foreign culture who will
play an integral role in interpreting communications, information,
goal setting, and implementation. He will know what works and
what doesn't in that culture, how to gain buy-in (acceptance
within the culture of important ideas and decisions), and whether
it is even possible to do so. Having skills in both cultures will enable him to translate both sides' strategies and goals into some sem-
blance of a realistic plan.*

The home office has to recognize the constraints as well as the
opportunities in international markets, not only integrating local
product needs and management attitudes into their plans but also
adjusting their own perceptions of time, leadership, and reward—

---

* These issues are handled in my course, "Managing Globally" (see pages 239–40 for further details).

all of which are cultural norms. The omission of these critical perspectives increases the failure potential of international alliances.

Culture Clash: Making Shoes in China

One example of culture-based management differences involves an American company with operations in the People's Republic of China. The project is a Chinese joint venture that was developed in 1993 for the manufacture of shoes. The U.S. company is in the Hockeystick, high-growth stage of the life cycle. It is managed by an entrepreneur who is young (in his midthirties) and aggressive—the typical Warrior manager who resists process, lauds sales, and believes that his way is not only the best but generally the only way to do business. For the Americans, the project is high profile but not highest priority, and would probably fit the Market Extending characterization, and closer to Experimental than to Bet the Farm.

The Chinese collective that is the partner in the project is made up of a closely knit group of villagers in an area outside Beijing, a former farming community that is now actively involved in commerce. They have other joint ventures with firms from Taiwan, Japan, and Korea. The shoe venture is the only one in that area with a U.S. company.

The cooperative is an interesting mix of contradictions. First it is a Start-up, with the insecurities of all Start-ups but with the added wrinkle of cultural collectivism. The village and project manager is an Adventurer. He essentially runs a fiefdom, but with another cultural wrinkle, which is that decision making has to be by consensus. Although this sounds as if equality is the rule, what it really means in the Chinese context is that the opinions of the older members of the collective will be greatly respected, and the maintenance of intergroup harmony and avoidance of overt conflict in interpersonal relationships will predominate. The Adventurer and his group also have to build confidence in their partner, as well as their own ability to do the job required by the venture.

At some point, problems occur in the manufacturing process, and the product that is produced is not of good quality. A U.S. manager goes to China to investigate the problem. He spends only two hours in the village, devoting most of that time to explaining to the village and project manager the importance of quality, emphasizing how critical it is that the shoe hides be of matching quality and color. He expresses his displeasure with the fact that the production runs are already late and delivery schedules are slipping, and repeats again and again how important it is to bring the product in on time.

With that enthusiastic pep talk, the American manager considers that the problem has been well communicated and will consequently be solved. The next run, however, is equally flawed.

It is clear that the managerial style of order giving, the demands of time-based delivery, and the lack of understanding of how business is transacted and decisions are made in China have compounded the manager's problems. Frustrated, the young owner of the company decides to make a trip to China. He is convinced that his charismatic leadership skills, which have thus far inspired the team of young people who surround his U.S. operation, are all that are needed to set the situation right.

When he arrives, the whole village council is there to meet him. There is much whispered discussion in Chinese. The U.S. entrepreneur is eager to get on with business, as he has scheduled only half a day in the area, and he turns down the invitation to an evening banquet in his honor.

The venture, he finds, is at a standstill. Run after run of product is unacceptable. The U.S. company decides to pull out of China and instead to create a joint venture in Mexico, just a short drive from Los Angeles, where the company is located. They incur a substantial loss of time, capital, and market opportunity because of their failed venture in China. They are also convinced that quality could never be understood by the Chinese.

Had they learned the cultural rules of doing business in China, the U.S. entrepreneur and his company could have saved themselves a lot of aggravation and increased their Asian business substantially. They would have understood the Start-up insecurity and need for confidence building of the Chinese operation. By applying the Mindshift diagnostic tools to themselves they could perhaps have understood that their own personality characteristics made their style so individualistic. This, coupled with cultural understanding of the Chinese, might have helped the U.S. entrepreneurial company to understand that their behavior could be considered autocratic in the eyes of Chinese.

In applying the cultural dynamics of collectivism and femininity—the predominant cultural traits of the Chinese, who value relationships highly—the U.S. company might have appreciated that the village manager needed time to understand and convey concepts of value to his team. In addition, the company owner's time constraints (only half a day in the area) added to the likelihood that misunderstandings would occur. Collectivism requires an understanding of the importance of the group within the company as well as within the village and the society as a whole. Femininity requires an appreciation of harmony. A rushed trip featuring an autocratic lecture and set of instructions given in a speech to the assembled workers was contrary to both of these cultural characteristics.

Finally, the project personality of the venture for the Chinese was Experimental. When intercultural misunderstandings started to occur, the project's priority started to slip until it was even below that level.

Why was the project of such low priority for the Chinese? One of the reasons was that they were also doing business with the Korean, Taiwanese, and Japanese, all cultures where group and consensual values are important and who thus understand Chinese cultural norms. Even though the Chinese partners might have respected American entrepreneurship and marketing know-how, when they encountered cultural difficulties, they turned their resources and attention to the partnerships that were more comfortable, ventures with Asian cultures with whom they felt they had more in common.

The ultimate cultural misstep was made when the young and opinionated U.S. owner snubbed their invitation to get to know them better by means of a longer visit, a banquet, all the niceties that are valued greatly in a relationship-based culture.

The issues in this alliance were resolvable. It need not have failed. An awareness of the differences and a willingness on both sides to learn would have led to a more satisfactory ending.

The understanding of what it takes to get buy-in to any strategy will require cultural input. For example, in Sweden, one national cultural characteristic is to have a strong commitment and sense of identification with the corporate entity. This is helpful in understanding occasional managerial reluctance to do anything that might not fit directly with the corporate culture as well as the high level of commitment to the culture in place. Because of their geography and size, the Swedes have a fine appreciation of the intricacies of international trade and a command of English, which on the whole enables them verbally to excell beyond other non-English-speaking cultures. The fluency in English, though, does not change the national characteristics; in fact, the apparent commonality, based on ability to communicate, may cause even greater misunderstanding.

The language of negotiation and implementation of the alliance may be English, but the meaning, application, and expectation is culturally influenced—as will be seen in the following cautionary tale.

Culture Clash: Bringing Swedish Pharmaceuticals to the U.S.A.

A client called us in to assist in an alliance with a Swedish company. The alliance was in extremis. Unfortunately, we could not change the dynamics at that late hour. All we could do was suggest a reconfiguration strategy, suspecting that the acrimony was too far gone to allow for revival. The facts were as follows.

A large, international, U.S.-based pharmaceutical company, in the Mature and Consolidating phase with some characteristics of a Declining company in its corporate bureaucracy, entered into an alliance with a small Swedish company, a Start-up, but one with a difference: The investors in the Swedish company included a large pharmaceutical company that had a limited Mature and Consolidating influence on the Start-up's activities.

The initial meetings and contract development went well. The U.S. partner approached the project with enthusiasm. They were looking to the alliance to open up their market in a particular area of medical devices and diagnostics, and a technology developed by the Swedish firm was of interest to them. The Swedish company, on the other hand, saw the strength of the U.S. company as an enormous asset, especially the fact that they had experience and knowledge of how to negotiate and succeed in the FDA approval process. They wanted to penetrate the U.S. market and create a distribution network that would generate sales there.

The agreement was entered into in 1985. The U.S. company immediately swung into action, creating a new division and staffing it with scientists and planners. They did not create a joint implementation plan with the Swedes, but unilaterally decided on the composition of the team for the new division. The Swedish company made the classic mistake of thinking that the U.S. company, because of its size, reputation, and presence in the United States market, knew exactly what they were doing.

If a blueprint were mapped of the process, two failure points would be spotted at this critical stage: lack of cross-functional teams containing the talent necessary to achieve the goals of the parties, and misalignment of the partners' objectives.

The sad tale continued as failure compounded itself. The U.S. team, using the skills at which they excelled, immediately started to reengineer the Swedish product. (After all, it was their moral obligation as scientists to present the very "best" product to the market.) Delays ensued. The planners pushed the FDA application date further out, explaining that there was no point in presenting the voluminous paperwork until they were absolutely ready.

The Swedes were frustrated and concerned. Confrontation is a difficult approach for them to take, whereas in the United States, the "John Wayne" approach to negotiation is often preferred. This implies "shooting from the hip" and is an unplanned, poorly thought out approach in which one goes with an aggressive stance "developed" at the spur of the moment. It implies that someone must win and therefore someone else must lose. The Swedish style of negotiation is very different.

The Swedes, mildly, indicated their concern about the delays. The U.S. representatives explained that the reputation of the company was such that they could only present the highest-quality product with their imprint and scientific expertise to the FDA. Months went by. Finally the trust—which was still fragile, as it is in most alliances at their inception—was destroyed. The Swedes lost hope that the U.S. partner would ever bring the product to the market, and they called for dissolution of the relationship.

What went wrong? The problem can be analyzed both strategically and culturally.

First, looking at the Pyramid of Alliances, it is clear that there was a misalignment from the start. The Swedes were looking for a distribution partner who could obtain FDA approval and enter the market with widespread distribution. This is low on the pyramid and requires less capital, lower risk, and less use of human resources.

The U.S. company was quite capable of achieving that goal. However, they saw the alliance as being higher up on the Pyramid, as a joint research and development partnership in which they were assuming some of the risks of new product development with distribution only as a secondary part of the outcome. The staffing of the new division ensured that the focus would be on research rather than on marketing and sales. The capital they invested went into the development and staffing of the infrastructure of a new joint research and development venture, rather than into the development of a distribution network and the creation of sales.

The parties' goals were misaligned. If they'd planned their implementation steps jointly, they would have seen the problem, which was thrown into relief by the choice of inappropriate teams. But since the implementation plan was not jointly developed, the staffing problem wasn't spotted and an opportunity was missed to see the larger misunderstanding.

In addition, the project personality was Bet the Farm for the Swedish company, and furthermore, they were a Start-up. This meant that their willingness to wait for the U.S. company to bring the product to market was limited. Certainly they were more patient than the typical U.S. Start-up. But they needed to see market entry and a revenue increase within a fairly short period of time. The U.S. company, on the other hand, saw the project as Experimental. They did allocate resources to it for a defined period of time, but the resources were the wrong ones.

How these misalignments were handled has to do primarily with cultural miscommunication, both corporate and country.

The Swedish company had chosen the U.S. company because of its reputation and therefore assumed that it would know and understand what was necessary for entry in the U.S. market. When the wrong people to achieve that goal were appointed, two problems arose. The first was miscommunication from the Start-up to the Mature company. The Adventurer manager might have thought, "Whom do I tell that the team seems functionally unbalanced? Surely they know what they are doing—look how successful they've been. I'm certainly not going to get caught up in their process [remember, Adventurers are resistant to process]. We'd better wait and see. Besides, I have large institutional investors who've put their faith in the U.S. company and in me. I am told that I have a high sense of urgency and I don't want to ruin the relationship by pushing too hard. The FDA process is complicated and takes time. The best decision would be to wait."

The second problem was the cultural issue. The Adventurer might rationalize as follows: "We don't understand the American market. The U.S. company does. Why make a fuss? We'll let them know that we're concerned about the loss of a market window of opportunity. They understand marketing—all U.S. companies are very good at marketing." Here we see the stereotype of all U.S. companies as market savvy, and also a cultural reluctance to confront.

The Americans, for their part, saw gaining access to Swedish technology as the achievement of their primary goal. Obtaining FDA approval was something they intended to do, once they had examined and evaluated the technology. The staffing of the venture with only scientists and planners almost assured its failure. The addition of marketing executives would have changed the activities and focus of the U.S. joint venture.

The result was the complete breakdown of the relationship—no trust, no confidence, and loss of face and opportunity on all sides.

Migratory and Embedded Knowledge and Country Culture

Understanding the issue of cultural differences in the way information is communicated and applying these understandings is critical. The view of migratory and embedded knowledge stated in Chapter 5 (see page 122) must be qualified in a cross-cultural setting. Communication is governed by norms, but cross-cultural expectations are often vastly different regarding embedded and migratory knowledge transfer. This is because communication will be interpreted differently according to the rules of each culture. When you superimpose cultural issues on the fact that generally companies only value and negotiate for the migratory knowledge transfer, opportunities for misunderstandings leading to relationship failure are compounded.

In a number of projects with China, U.S. companies have discovered that the negotiated transaction, that is, the migratory knowledge, is rarely the Chinese partner's motivation for the partnership. The embedded knowledge generally has the greatest value for them.

Misunderstandings can occur in China-U.S. joint ventures when the U.S. partner states its goals clearly, namely, access to the Chinese market, whereas the Chinese partner approaches the relationship more indirectly and keeps its real agenda hidden. If the U.S. company is inexperienced in doing business in that region, they may resist the Chinese approach, which is that a great deal of information must first be transferred to them by the U.S. partner, especially embedded knowledge, before they will enter into a long-term commitment.

The Chinese look at a contract as only a part of an ongoing and continuous negotiation, as more entities, individuals, and opportunities enter into and change the dynamics of the original situation.

Unintended Knowledge Transfer to China

A U.S. company's failure to grasp the realities of doing business in China caused much dissatisfaction in the U.S. organization with the speed of their goal achievement. The deliverables (what it was agreed would be the migratory-information goal for the parties) deadline date for the project kept changing, and this constant redefinition of the partnership goals diminished the U.S. company's original enthusiasm for the project. Their original goal, market access, seemed to retreat further and further away, and the growth of administrative problems added to their discontent. The transfer of embedded knowledge also led to a strong feeling of being taken advantage of. For example, a continuing stream of Chinese representatives came to visit the U.S. company in the States—the trip financed by the U.S. partner—and received detailed demonstrations and explanations of manufacturing and management processes.

The rules of engagement had clearly been misunderstood, and we stated our view that the situation required a serious re-examination by the U.S. partner as to whether they wanted to become further involved in doing business in China at this time, or whether other emerging countries would be better suited to their way of doing business. The U.S. partner decided gradually to withdraw resources from the Chinese project and move them to India, where doing business with one of the key families in the region meant that they could limit the knowledge transfer predominantly to migratory knowledge.

The individuals who represented the Indian family inter-ests were Western-educated, spoke excellent English, and were highly sophisticated. The U.S. executives felt "comfort-able." And so they should. Their Indian partners had tran-scended the cultural barriers to relate to them in a way they could recognize, negotiating and implementing contracts in a Western, overt and direct way. Clearly, the Americans were not ready to do business in China. This is an example where attractive international market opportunities existed but the U.S. company, an exporter, lacked cultural flexibility. Realiza-tion of that fact saved them from entering on a drawn-out process of trying to do business in China when the corporate commitment was not there to do what would be necessary to succeed in that market.

The next chapter takes the significant body of knowledge that you and your company have accumulated in following the alliance-planning process thus far, and channels it into imple-mentation and management of the alliance.

7.
Implementing and Managing the Alliance

If you have followed the steps described in Chapters 1 through 6, you have been developing the fundamentals of the alliance-implementation plan. You have also been learning the critical issues of alliance management: evaluation of goals, refining communication, selecting team members, setting reasonable expectations, and many other factors that arise in the planning stages but are equally important in the alliance-management process. If you have examined these factors and developed your organizational, customized approach, the actual management of the alliance will hold far fewer surprises.

Now it's time to formalize your alliance-implementation, or operating, plan, working jointly with your partner. The plan will generally be a written document, its formality level dependent on the personality of the companies involved. In it specific attention will be devoted to staffing, resources allocation, monitoring of the alliance, expectations, and financial considerations. In the development of this document as well as in the ongoing relationship, it is more important to develop mutual problem-solving skills than it is to battle for or capitulate on a particular position. Problems will continue to arise, so logical, candid discussion and negotiation of compromises with your partner in the constantly changing context of the ongoing relationship are essential. At all times you should treat the partner with the same care and respect you would give a customer.

Questions that should be answered in the document include the following:

- Who will do what?
- How will contributions be made?
- What time constraints and milestones can be agreed on now?
- What communications mechanisms will be in place for approvals?
- How will the information flow?
- Who will be the liaison from each company?
- What incentive programs are appropriate?
- How will the partnership fit with the existing relationships of both companies?

Part of the implementation plan must be a process to keep your partner informed on all alliance-related activities, both positive and negative developments. Criticism is important, but it is most helpful when it is coupled with positive affirmation of the areas of the relationship that are functioning as planned. For this give-and-take to occur, it is important that the lines of communication be known to the alliance implementors, and that they be open and growing.

The implementation plan will also outline both partners' expectations. These need to be consistent and aligned in order for partners to feel that they are gaining appropriate responses from the other side. Inconsistencies will become evident in this stage if they haven't before. If a fundamental inconsistency shows up, it may indicate a deeper problem, as described in the case of the Swedish–U.S. pharmaceuticals alliance in Chapter 6.

By this time the alliance manager should have been selected. If the alliance has defined a series of smaller projects that are needed to achieve its overall objectives, then various subproject managers and team members should also have been designated. All members should be clear on the project goals and how they relate to other projects that are within the alliance, as well as the scope of the projects in terms of the Mindshift project-personality categories: Experimental, Market Extending, or Bet the Farm. Priorities should be clearly set and agreed upon.

Scenario Building

Scenario building is an important tool in creating the alliance implementation and operating plan. In scenario building, both partners participate in simulations of what-ifs that could happen during the partnership. The importance of the scenario-building process is that it is risk-free, since none of the scenario conditions and events have happened yet. In a scenario-building exercise it is reasonable and safe to ask the kinds of questions that might not be asked in a real-life situation, for example, "Who would manage this process if Joe left?" or "If XYZ company enters the market, we'll have a major competitor to deal with. What will our contingency plan be?" or "If the technology misses the deadline for completion, how would we deal with that?" and so on.

Until now you have been approaching the alliance from an external perspective, that is, with each company's strategies and goals in mind; in scenario building you are moving over to an internal perspective regarding the integrity of the details of the alliance itself. The specifics of the project goals and how they will be achieved under differing sets of circumstances must be spelled out.

Another important part of scenario building, which is also part of the ongoing management of the alliance, is the creation of standards for project reporting and documentation. It should be understood how the alliance managers will respond to requests for information from a senior manager such as "How is the project doing? Can you send me an update?" or to a more detailed demand for specifics of project research that is under way and how they are meeting project milestones or goals. Here differences in corporate personality must be taken into account, especially in R&D projects. Sloppy reporting techniques—leading to problems later on—can be forestalled by reaching an agreement at this stage on reporting standards for alliance projects.

Another critical issue that must be addressed in scenario building and included in management techniques for an alliance, is project communication structures: the way managers of projects will communicate with each other and with their home companies.

Tangled Lines of Communication and Responsibility

One alliance had a very complicated project communication structure that, when untangled, revealed hidden inconsistencies in the partners' expectations for the alliance.

There were two alliance managers, one from each company, as well as project managers for each of the subprojects who reported to the alliance managers. The idea was that the alliance managers would act as troubleshooters and liaison people between the two companies but would not get involved in the specifics of the projects unless they ran into trouble.

Both the alliance managers and the project managers, however, also had ongoing responsibilities for various nonalliance activities that consumed a healthy percentage of their time. For these activities they reported to others within their own companies. This produced problems of empowerment, authority, and time management, all combined with conflicting loyalties and responsibilities. The alliance and project managers could not allocate the appropriate amount of time, loyalty, and attention to the alliance and there was an ongoing conflict of nonalliance with alliance responsibilities. The result was that the alliance got short shrift and was eventually resented by the whole team from both companies, since it was seen as pulling them away from the "real work" they all had to perform. This issue was one that would have immediately raised a red flag had a scenario-building technique been used. The managers would have mentally walked through the process of divided priorities in their scenario discussions and in the process the inconsistencies would have become clear, and another reporting and responsibility structure (such as a dedicated alliance team) could have been chosen.

Our advice was to start by examining whether the trust factor had dissipated to the extent that the alliance was unsalvageable. If it had not, then we recommended that the alliance be restructured so that a single manager, selected by the joint team from both companies, would manage the project. Conflict resolution would be handled by a committee of three from each company.

We also discovered an inconsistency between the stated and actual project personality. The project scope was clearly lower than Experimental to both companies in the way they were allocating resources, even though the CEOs indicated it was Bet the Farm. This inconsistency—the CEOs said the project was critical but did not allocate the resources to support such a project personality—was one of the factors that was destroying the trust factor between the two companies. Scenario building prior to entering into the alliance or in its initial stages would have highlighted this issue as well as the reporting and responsibility structure. Project communication problems were just the tip of the iceberg in this instance; ultimately this problem area led to a complete reevaluation of the viability of the entire alliance.

Another lesson here is the fact that inspirational leadership in an alliance is not enough. The CEOs both had a vision of the potential of the alliance between these two companies, but they did not translate that inspired vision to the operating managers in a way that empowered them to allocate the resources or make the organizational changes to manage the alliance effectively.

Scenario building is often an enjoyable and interesting exercise for both sides. It can also be very revealing. Be sure that you get input from cross-functional groups within the company when you design your scenario variables. For example, if only marketing people are involved, you will derive benefit from their point of view but might miss what someone in research or manufacturing could contribute.

Scenario building can also be incorporated much earlier in the planning process, even before any partner has been selected. Your company may want to try a scenario-building exercise using hypothetical partners, applying various premises regarding performance, contribution, market changes, technology delays, and myriad other contingencies that could change the dynamics or success potential of a partnership. After the team gets further into the process, you can insert the actual company facts and names in order to continue to build reality into the process of creating a scenario in which you can work together.

Ongoing Management of the Changing Alliance

A critical issue that must be agreed upon at the start of the alliance is what constitutes success for the alliance as a whole. In addition, you may wish to have an internal document, confidential to your organization, that defines success in your corporate terms. However, remember that "success" is a moving target. You may change your success criteria as the partnership matures.

Redefining Success

A U.S. company that had been in an alliance with a British company for three years realized that the underlying circumstances of both companies had changed, and so had the market.

The U.S. company was an entrepreneurial supplier of equipment that had joined in a distribution agreement with the British company. When that the relationship began, the U.S. company had had no sales in Europe. Three years later, they not only had the British distributor but also their own sales offices throughout Europe.

The British distributor was a family-owned company, $500 million in size, with an excellent reputation. They specialized in large-system sales, whereas the U.S. company product was in the small-systems area. The British salespeople resented selling small systems, when for the same effort they could sell a larger and more expensive system and obtain a sizable commission.

We first verified that the market was growing and worth the effort of reconfiguring the alliance. Then we worked with the European country managers, deriving critical information for the U.S. company that led them, on our recommendation, to create a different management structure in the United States, one that was more responsive to European requirements. We assisted them to create a new European strategic plan, developed from the country level upward.

The alliance managers in the U.S. company were also given a different perspective of cross-cultural management issues, and some management changes took place in order to move the right people into those sensitive positions. The right people were those who had cross-cultural understanding and could handle the stress and ambiguity of the changing nature of a growing market and a reconfigured alliance. This was immensely gratifying to the American company's European country managers, who had become very frustrated with the lack of response from U.S.-dominated research and manufacturing departments to the European requests for product changes.

Finally, we helped both partners put a different structure to the alliance. The British company created an OEM (original equipment manufacturer) relationship with the U.S. company, using their equipment technology in the large-system design, but leaving small-system sales to the U.S. company's own sales team in Europe. The alliance continued with a new definition of success for each partner.

Strategic alliances go through cycles of formation and change, as depicted in Figure 7-1, "The Continuing Strategic Partnership Cycle."

Figure 7-1: The Continuing Strategic Partnership Cycle

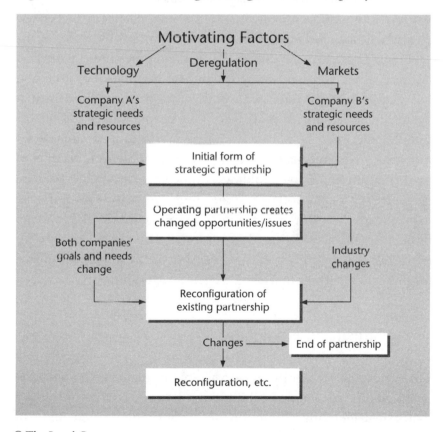

Organizational Attitude to the Alliance

Alliance managers face a continuing challenge to create an environment that can respond to the needs and changing requirements not only of the alliance but also of senior management in each of the alliance partners. Internal project needs may require changing the resources that have been allocated, moving people around who are not functioning well in their roles, and other project-management skills. There is also the added complication of keeping a commitment to learn from the partnering organization while not transferring knowledge that has not been contracted for. This adds a dimension of stress to normal project management tasks.

One of the most difficult situations for an alliance manager occurs when unrealistic pressures are put upon him by senior management. These may be due to stock market pressures or internal political issues. Alliances started with one premise of expectation for success that are vested with political or financial burdens that occur after the alliance is in place can be put under intolerable strain. Sometimes the only way to deal with this is to educate senior executives internally by comparing the potential benefits of market positioning and building competitive advantage that are characteristic of the long-term and high-risk nature of some alliances with the short-term nature of other kinds of corporate projects or alliances that are lower on the Pyramid of Alliances. It is possible that an organization with a short-term approach is inappropriate as a partner in a longer-term relationship.

Stress and Ambiguity

One of the characteristics most valuable in managers of alliances is the ability to handle ambiguity and stress. By definition, alliance managers must function on a continuum of change—of company goals for each partner, of market and industry goals, possibly in a multitude of jurisdictions—and will be balancing the intricacies of changing managerial goals. As seen in Figure 7-1, a continuing alliance relationship is defined by the desires of both parties to terminate or carry on with the partnership. Reconfiguration of a troubled relationship may keep it going, but only if both partners want that result and proactively work toward it.

Vanishing Brainpower

In one case, an acquisition—a type of alliance at the top of the Pyramid of Alliances, since it requires greater cost and human resource allocation and risk—caused a result opposite to what both companies wanted. Company A acquired Company B in hopes of seizing a leadership position in the biotechnology industry. As part of the acquisition there was substantial downsizing in Company B's human-resource, accounting, and finance areas. Interpreting this as the new state of affairs, most of the biotech scientists in Company B found themselves other jobs.

All of this happened fairly quickly. Since the acquiring company was a Declining one, their processes of communication were slow and laborious. They did not convey a strong and clear message to the scientists that the reason for their acquisition was so that the biotech genius within the organization could be used to the integrated company's benefit. The acquired company was in the Hockeystick stage and its founders intended to stay in the company for some time. The rest of the R&D team, however, never really understood that they were the very reason for the acquisition. The acquiring company ended up with higher debt and limited intellectual assets as they saw their key scientists disappearing through the company door.

More Alliance Success Factors

Continued Reexamination of the Alliance

Another issue that is constantly evaluated during the life of alliances that are not acquisitions, especially if there are dramatic market and industry changes, is the cost-benefit analysis. Does the benefit of the alliance outweigh the cost of participation? It is when the costs outweigh the benefits that alliance structures start to fracture.

Other questions that must be asked are, Is the alliance achieving the return on investment—the strategic migratory, contracted and embedded, implicit goals of the partners? If not, whether this is recognized by the partners or not, the relationship will start to suffer from the stresses of nonperformance or misaligned expectations.

Does the alliance conform to its business plan? Is teamwork an issue? Are there leadership or champion problems? Is conflict resolution being well handled? Might there be a need for internal mentoring? What is the consensus regarding strategic fit—is the alliance still the "right" one?

Some companies also use a confidential team-assessment tool, applied every six months or annually. Each member fills it out and evaluates his or her perception of the alliance, how it is or isn't working and the participation of particular team members in it. This performance-evaluation process is used for continuous improvement. It is a useless exercise unless changes are implemented. This is where the team, working with corporate staff, must apply the results and even tackle political sacred cows in order to remake the alliance if necessary.

We recommend a regular review of alliance achievements every three to six months. This is important both for the alliance team members, and as a communication tool to the other members of both organizations. It is not uncommon for the alliance team members to be pleased with the alliance progress, only to find that senior management, because of poor internal communication, is under the impression that "nothing is happening."

You may remember the "internal approval" discussion earlier in the book (see page 130). Internal approval has to continue, now in a metamorphosed form, as "internal updates." If those non–decision-makers who could have pulled the plug on the emerging alliance earlier are not kept apprised of alliance activity throughout the relationship, they can cause problems again. Furthermore, it is good business practice for senior management in all partner companies to be familiar with the progress of alliance activity.

Continued Upgrading of Alliance Managerial Skills

Alliance managers must constantly be on the lookout for ways to upgrade their skills. One way to facilitate this is the "best practices" approach. Introduce the best managers in both companies to each other; many of these may be the very people who are breaking new ground in the alliance-management area, and as the field of experience grows, there is much to be shared. You may also want to try "alliance benchmarking": set up visits for executives to visit various companies that are managing alliances competently, in order for them to increase their skills and expand their perspectives.

Because this area of expertise is growing rapidly, some organizations have seen the need to integrate the planning for alliances into the general strategic planning process, as a parallel activity. This is logical and saves time. It means that as the organization is developing its domestic or international strategic plan, it can select the alliance option as an appropriate one. But those who do, will need to speed up the alliance planning process, making it part of the strategic planning approach rather than a consequence of it.

Teamwork as a Success Factor

Companies that have developed internal processes for good teamwork and communication between corporate-level business-development or alliance staffs and the operating managers who have ultimate profit-and-loss responsibility for the alliance are generally able to implement and manage alliances more successfully than those where there is tension between corporate-level and operations managers. As seen in one of the earlier case studies, the typical result of an adversarial relationship between corporate staff and the groups or divisions where the alliance will be located is that no operating manager will want responsibility for or ownership of the project.

Integration of Alliance Results into the Organization

Many organizations fail to leverage the benefits of their alliances, as a result of inadequate internal communication mechanisms or of characteristics of their corporate, managerial, or project personalities. A few companies have developed an internal education approach that continually exposes those within the company who are not directly involved in the alliance to its results. One company that has a number of research and development alliances holds an annual internal conference for technology development, which brings together many of their technology experts from all activities of the $20 billion organization and where particular areas can be showcased.

Managing alliances will test even the most competent of executives. The capabilities involved will include not only careful planning and implementation, but also a broad perspective and an open mind. Chapter 8 gives you a glimpse into the future world of alliances.

8.
A View of the Future World of Alliances

In the first chapter we defined an alliance philo-
sophically and structurally. In this final chapter, it is time to rise
above the nuts and bolts of alliance relationship management and
to reflect on some of the macro issues that must be taken into account by all businesses and especially by parties in alliance creation.
By macro issues, I mean those involving the world beyond our
own companies, industries, countries, and even the world beyond
our life span. As part of this process, shift your mind into a different gear and consider information in cycles of decades, even cen-
turies. In doing this, we'll draw upon the work of scientists, a
futurist, an economist, and financial consultants, and from their
views we will extrapolate the applications that I see for the world
of alliances.

In this chapter I spin a number of concepts into the mix and at the
end of it all, pull them into a coherent approach that will broaden
some perceptions. The concepts under review are as follows:

- *What it means to be a global company; How this affects alliances*
- *"Small is good"—the impact of this view on alliances*
- *Technology fusion*
- *From virtuality to reality*
- *Economic change and alliances*
- *Business reengineering and alliances*

What It Means to Be a Global Company; How This Affects Alliances

In keeping with the trend toward globalization, many American companies now consider themselves to be multinationals and call themselves global. Apart from semantic precision, there are practical reasons for getting the definitions straight and accurately understanding how your organization is positioned on the scale that moves from 100 percent domestic to 100 percent global.

The Ernst & Young survey of CEOs cited in Chapter 1 (see pages 21–22) gave helpful definitions of "domestic," "exporter," "transnational," and "global" companies, which I have slightly modified as follows:[1]

A *domestic* company conducts all manufacturing and selling in one country.

An *exporter* company has sales in many countries and conducts strategic decision making from its home country.

A *transnational* company manufactures and sells according to an integrated plan encompassing countries of a region.

A *global* company has sales worldwide and conducts strategic decision making outside the home country.

On the basis of these definitions, survey participants were asked to characterize their organizations and compare their view of their company five years ago, in the present, and five years hence. A majority of the companies saw their organizations transitioning into transnationals and global operators and confirmed that they would be using alliances as the methodology to assist them in their international expansion. Of course, as with any survey, the answers given by executives regarding their own companies' global status must be qualified by their lack of objectivity. In my experience few companies are actually "global" although their executives describe them as such.

These definitions are useful to an organization for the specific purpose of pinpointing where strategic, and therefore possibly alliance, decision making will take place. If you are a U.S. company partnering with a Japanese company that calls itself global but whose decision making takes place at headquarters in Tokyo, you are dealing with a company that may essentially be an exporter. In the planning stage of an alliance, the getting-to-know-you period, the locus of decision making is one of the questions that must be asked and answered. Otherwise you may make significant miscalculations regarding how long it will take to get program approval, make product changes, even act on budgetary amendments—the time needed for all of these may be vastly underestimated. Do not be misled by a word. Look behind the semantics for the information that discloses the real culture of the company.

Whether the label "global" is really appropriate is not always a simple determination.

A "Global" Company: True or False?

We have had many debates with one of our clients that is 50 percent owned by an Asian company on the subject of globalism and multifaceted, multicultural decision making. Although the credo of the U.S. company was to empower managers to make decisions, the reality was different. In fact, decision making was controlled at the top of what was a hierarchical company. The Asian company was clearly centrally controlled. The success of the ten-year alliance had depended on the goodwill and understanding of the two CEOs, one in Asia and the other in the United States. Both companies had far-flung, successful, and intricate international operations, called themselves global and discussed the importance of input of country managers. But the bottom line was that they were both exporters. Local and country general managers understood this. They made allowances for consensus decision making and the time it took on the Asian side, and the lack of in-depth research and the drive to enter a fast-changing market on the U.S. side. The dissimilar approaches were computed into every decision and its implementation, and compromise was reached. There were few misconceptions about where the real power resided in each organization. As a result, the alliance worked well. What came out in our discussions was that the U.S. managers wanted an end to the pretense of a collaborative, multilocal, decentralized organization.

"Let's call it what it is," one manager complained. "We all know who makes the decisions around here. We waste so much time giving lip service to team decision making and consensus building. It seems to work all right the way it is. Why are we trying to become a collaborative organization when everyone knows we're not?"

Some companies struggle long and hard to change into global operators. In the consumer-products area, a number of organizations have turned themselves upside down, with the customer at the head of the information flow and all global decisions driven by that local understanding. That means that they have created local product modifications, service changes, tailored niche promotions, advertising, employee incentives and reward systems, plus myriad other business processes to fit the cultural environment.

The Reins Remain in Europe

Little progress could be made with one particular alliance, of a large European multi-billion-dollar energy industry company and a smaller U.S. organization with $200 million in revenues. The European company, headquartered in Munich, presented itself as global and emphasized that its strategic decision making took place around the world. The reality became clear in one project among many the two companies were working on. The need arose to create a way to reward and provide incentives to a group of employees who were working night and day on innovative new technology. The senior management of the U.S. company suggested that each company create a phantom stock plan, which would reward the individual efforts of managers of both the German and the U.S. companies, allowing them to "share" in the increased good fortunes of the venture. The larger company was unable to modify its incentive system because of certain corporate policies and procedures that were a function of their country culture: Their European culture did not reward entrepreneurship, instead favoring loyalty to the larger group and organization. The smaller, U.S.-based company readily agreed to the suggestion. Thus even though the strategic opportunity dictated a change in policy for the European company that was appropriate for this entrepreneurial venture, the real location of decision making became clear. It was in Germany.

All the employees of the venture, regardless of country culture, were disappointed when no agreement on compensation tied to increased value of the venture could be reached. All of them had heard of the great rewards from stock appreciations that individual entrepreneurs had reaped in the United States. However, it was not to be.

One solution suggested by the smaller company was to spin the project off into a separate entity in which both groups of employees could be equally vested and rewarded.

The staid larger company, which was Mature and Consolidating, rejected that proposal. The smaller company, which was a high-growth, Hockeystick-stage company, could not understand why such a plan couldn't be worked out. After all, all the employees were in favor of it, the project would not only meet but was expected to far exceed the original projected return on investment (ROI) for both entities, and it would be consistent with the mutual goals of integrated system development for both companies as an industry standard. But the larger organization's country and corporate culture dominated management's thinking and they remained opposed to the concept. It would pit individual employee interests against the protection of the corporate persona, and from their long-term perspective, ROI as a value did not supersede corporate integrity. The corporation was seen to be an entity that serves a greater good than that of a few individuals, namely, the good of the community, providing long-term and steady employment, not encouraging individual entrepreneurship.

Unfortunately, the project began to lose momentum; what had been a special opportunity for a major breakthrough in their respective industries began to disappear. Damage control is in place, but it is increasingly difficult to keep the excitement and commitment of the technologists at its former high level.

A possible solution for this relationship might be a cross-licensing arrangement with bonuses related to performance. This will not be the "big kill" that both employee groups were hoping for, but it would be better than nothing and would preserve the corporate and community interests of the one partner while rewarding the ROI expectations and individual efforts of both groups of employees.

In any case, what was highlighted by the search for an incentive was that the German company was an exporter company, with some elements of a transnational, no matter what its executives said; the U.S. company's image of it as a global company was altered by the reality of decision making taking place at European headquarters in Munich.

The moral of the story is, that when you are forming an alliance, it is imperative that the actual location of strategic decision making be discovered early on in the process of relationship development, in order to save time and avoid complications later.

"Small Is Good"—The Impact of This View on Alliances

The futurist John Naisbitt presents the concept of empowering small units to be stronger, and he draws an analogy with the world of computers: the change from the mainframe computer to PCs networked together. He states, "The bigger the world economy, the more powerful its smallest players. . . . The entrepreneur is also the most important player in the building of the global economy. So much so that big companies are decentralizing and reconstituting themselves as networks of entrepreneurs."[2]

Certainly many companies are empowering small units to be stronger, but in cultures that value the group over the individual, where this trend goes against the cultural norm, change comes more slowly.

The Japanese have evolved a unique angle on the decentralization movement. The soaring value of the yen (from 125 yen to the dollar in 1993 to 80 in 1995) and a sagging domestic economy have caused numerous smaller Japanese manufacturers to set up shop in Bangkok, Manila, Beijing, and Singapore. This infusion into other Asian countries of key building blocks of Japan's manufacturing structure—the small manufacturers that are an integral element of the Japanese system of affiliated business groups (called *keiretsu*)—brings not only jobs but technology. It is also reducing the massive amounts of Japanese imports into East Asia.

Small manufacturers in Japan generally have fewer than three hundred workers and capitalization of less than $1 million. By 1992 estimates, such small companies were producing more than 52 percent of Japan's industrial output. They are also a cost buffer for the larger manufacturers, since their wages are lower. One example of the relationship between these small companies and Japan's manufacturing giants could be seen when TDK Corporation moved the manufacturing operation for its magnetic tape operations from Japan to Malaysia: One of its suppliers, Dai-Ichi Kaken Koyogo, a tiny plastic components manufacturer with forty workers in Japan's Yamanashi prefecture, followed them. Using Malaysian government incentives such as tax deferrals, Dai-Ichi Kaken Koyogo set up a manufacturing venture of invested capital for just $400,000, a fraction of what the cost would have been in Japan. The money was spent mostly on production equipment brought from Japan. As a result, Dai-Ichi kept TDK Corp's business and reduced their own ongoing manufacturing costs by 40 percent.

Now Indonesia, Thailand, and Malaysia are sending regular missions of domestic companies to Japan to seek partners. Since Asian countries have been trading partners for generations, there already exist some mutual understandings. Nevertheless, the intercultural challenges they will face within the next ten years will be critical, and the intricacies of alliances and changing mutual interests will require the use of many advanced management tools in order to keep the economic bonds secure.

Inevitably there will be both successes and failures among individual alliances, but the trend is toward emancipation of the Asian region's producers of parts and components—as John Naisbitt predicted—and in cultures where the group perspective has traditionally dominated the interests of the individual.[3]

As the trend toward decentralization continues, the next stage in alliance development in the upcoming decade will have to do with multilocal, multicultural complexities. The focus at many companies will change from finding partners or defining process and methodology to *managing from a decentralized perspective, pushing management control to a local level.* It will take a mature and secure senior management with international expertise and sophistication to encourage such an environment.

Technology Fusion

Alliances play an important role in the area of technology development. One of the principle issues concerns the advantages of "technology fusion." Fumio Kodama, professor at Saitama University's Graduate School of Policy Science in Japan, in an article for the *Harvard Business Review* titled "Technology Fusion and the New R&D," states:

> No longer can companies afford to miss a generation of technology and remain competitive. . . . Either a company can invest in R&D that replaces an older generation of technology—the "breakthrough approach"—or it can focus on combining existing technologies into hybrid technologies—the "technology fusion" approach. The former is a linear, step-by-step strategy of technology substitution . . . [for example,] the CD replaced the record album. Technology fusion, on the other hand, is non-linear, complementary and cooperative. It blends incremental technical improvements from several previously separate fields of technology to create products that revolutionize markets. For example, marrying optics and electronics created opto-electronics, which gave birth to fiber-optics communications systems."[4]

Factors for change—such as the shortening of product life cycles and innovations that cross industry boundaries—lead to the technology fusion approach. The market drives R&D agendas and forces them to become demand-driven. Intelligence gathering of innovations occurs *outside the organization's industry.* In spite of the advantages, Kodama alleges, many Western companies still rely on the breakthrough approach for reasons that include a not-invented-here engineering arrogance, whereas in Japan technology fusion is strongly implemented by companies such as Nippon Telephone and Telegraph, Fanuc, NEC, and others.

It is outside the industry that opportunity for alliances must be highlighted. Even if your organizational culture leads you to believe that acquisitions are the only appropriate alliance structure, you should consider the area of technology fusion as a competitive opportunity. It lends itself to R&D consortia and to joint ventures that are reciprocal and have substantial commitment of resources combined with a long-term approach. Clearly countries with cooperative research consistent with industrial policy, such as Japan, may be culturally and legally (because of the lack of the restraint of antitrust laws) more open to cooperative opportunities.

Nevertheless, in the United States cooperative consortia in some industries have gone a long way toward achieving technology fusion. In the semiconductor world, a number of leading semiconductor manufacturers formed a consortium called SEMICON, and in the computer industry, the leading computer manufacturers formed Micro Electronics and Computer Technology Corporation (MCC) in Austin, Texas.

Individual companies should at the very least be scanning other industries for what I call "the invisible competitor," a company which is active in another industry and would not be easily discovered in the normal competitive analysis. Invisible competitors are a factor in the messy, promising overlap of the telecommunications, entertainment, and multimedia industries, where it is increasingly difficult to know where industry boundaries lie. The telephone companies have lost their captive market since theirs is no longer the only direct line that accesses the households of millions around the world and "invisible competitors" are emerging every day.

From Virtuality to Reality

The most extreme example of the shift from internal control to multilocal, external, and alliance relationships is the *virtual corporation*. This is not one company but rather a group of companies that come together in interconnected networks of alliances for mutual benefit. Although this concept has been much discussed, no more than a few organizations today have characteristics of such an entity; these are mainly in the entertainment industry, with some in construction management of complex projects. Each project involves a different constellation of companies joined together by a common goal, each providing its core competency to the project.

It is clear that more virtual corporations will evolve, but it will be a long time until they are the norm rather than the exception.

The goal of the virtual corporation is to deliver to the customer the lowest-cost, highest-value product that the entire value chain (not just a single company) can produce. The theory is that through cooperative effort the virtual enterprise manages the total value chain through a series of alliances with suppliers, manufacturers, distributors, and others. In such an enterprise, ownership of internal processes must give way to collaboration and communication, and direct management and control yield to shared responsibilities and goals.

The virtual corporation will require a major paradigm shift in the core company strategic direction, as companies move from vertical integration to collaboration and outsourcing. However, it is dangerous to "outsource" and equally risky to develop any alliances until you know and have clearly identified your organization's core competency. Only this way will you prevent the "deskilling" of your company.

Along the path to virtuality, the first step is a reevaluation of the business processes and strategies that are being used to develop, manufacture, market, and sell your products and services to their distributors and ultimate consumers. Many of these processes may not be core competencies and therefore could be outsourced, freeing up resources for activities that are critical to the maintenance of your organization's competitive advantage.

Economic Change and Alliances

Professor John D. Sterman, director of the System Dynamics Group of the Sloan School of Management of the Massachusetts Institute of Technology, in a presentation to the Bank Credit Analysts Conference in New York in September 1992, discussed the sixty-year process of the economic long-wave theory according to which there is a forty- to sixty-year economic cycle that is separate from the business cycle. Sterman separated economic activity into four modes, graphically illustrated in Figure 8-1, "Modes of Economic Activity."

He explained that the most relevant of all the modes to explain long-term economic developments is the long-wave cycle. Combining the long-wave and the business cycles produces the results depicted in Figure 8-2, "The Long-Wave and Business Cycles."

In essence, Professor Sterman's theory is that

> during the long wave upswing, the business cycle expansions will be long and strong because the economy is rising up on the long wave. Recessions tend to be short and shallow. . . . The opposite occurs when the long wave peaks and begins to decline. The business cycle will appear to have changed with long deep recessions and weak recoveries. . . . If we do not recognize the presence of the long wave, the transition from the upswing to the downswing produces confusion, anxiety, pessimism and a crisis of confidence.[5]

Professor Sterman further infers that

> the long wave is so large and slow that the pressures it creates cannot be accommodated within a market system that focuses only on the short term. These pressures spill out beyond the confines of the

Figure 8-1: Modes of Economic Activity

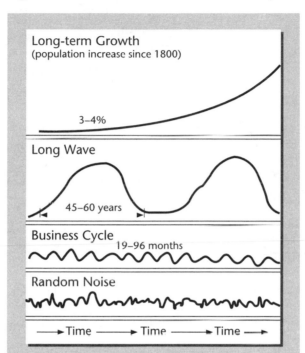

Long-term Growth
(population increase since 1800)

3–4%

Long Wave

45–60 years

Business Cycle
19–96 months

Random Noise

Time ——— Time ——— Time

© Professor J. D. Sterman

economic system into the political and social arena. . . . Changes in the "structure" of the world system are in many cases the result of the stresses generated by the downswing of the long wave. They are far more important than the strength and timing of the next business cycle recovery; they will shape the world we live in for the next two generations.

The next extension of Professor Sterman's theory is into the area of the political implications of the long wave, which he derived from studies of "content analysis" of conservative versus liberal phraseologies. These are summarized in Figure 8-3, "Political Implications of the Long Wave."

Figure 8-2: The Long-Wave and Business Cycles

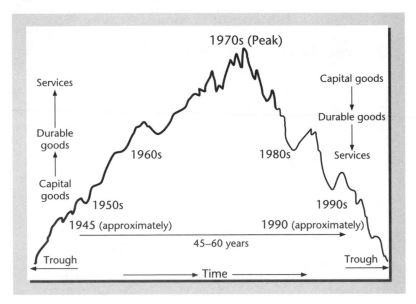

Hypothetical graph showing the interaction of the business cycle, the long wave, and random events. During the long-wave upswing, recessions are short and mild. During the downswing, recessions are long and deep.

© Professor J. D. Sterman

Professor Sterman predicts that the late 1990s will be the peak for the "parochial" phase of political thought and activity—in which protectionist thinking holds sway. If in the late 1990s we are experiencing the trough of long wave, and with it a rise in parochialism, then knowledge of local customs and markets is vital. If protectionism is rife, then we must be part of or have access to the "in-group," with local understandings and cultural and language skills. If a decision is to be made between developing a wholly owned operation or entering into a joint venture with a local partner, economic trends in this decade are mandating the latter.

We are in a time when new technologies, new management methods, and general discontinuity open the doors for doing

Figure 8-3: Political Implications of the Long Wave

Economy	Politics
Expansion	Progressive (social justice and enfranchisement, e.g., civil rights)
Peak	Cosmopolitan (international trade and foreign affairs)
Decline	Conservative (domestic issues, smaller government, anti–civil rights)
Trough	Parochial (people out for themselves, protectionist, e.g., fascism)

© Professor J. D. Sterman

things differently, uniquely, creatively. Other immediate strategies that strategically fit the point in the long-wave economic cycle that we are at include joint ventures to acquire or develop new approaches and technologies; licensing to local partners with market know-how; distribution and joint marketing agreements with local partners to overcome international protectionism; reinventing the corporation in order to respond to individual needs, with customized services using new approaches of interactive media, hybrid technology, and crossover of industries.

Another side of protectionism is the reverse brain drain that is now beginning to accelerate in the United States. Korean, Indian, Russian, and Chinese technologists, who have obtained their postgraduate training and often fairly extensive business experience in the United States, are returning to their homelands with cash and knowledge in hand. This trend represents a major opportunity to develop alliances with managers in overseas locations, who have cultural familiarity with U.S. management methods and perspectives and can act as a liaisons for U.S. management. (In some instances a manager who has returned to his home country may not necessarily have the confidence of his countrymen in a large organization, and in fact may be resented for his overseas sojourn.) These young managers take with them the spirit of entrepreneurship and a network of contacts. In very recent times, the foreign-educated local managers have been joined by Americans who are refugees of downsizing and corporate cutbacks.

When these movements are considered with the larger perspective of Professor Sterman's view, it is clear that companies that can draw managers who possess cross-cultural acceptance and understanding will be the ones that manage well through the trials of the trough of the long-wave cycle and will be poised to profit from the upswing of the next recovery cycle.

Business Reengineering and Alliances

Finally, a comment needs to be made on the relationship of alliances to the concept of business reengineering. Michael Hammer, one of the concept's chief architects, defines reengineering as follows:

> Re-engineering is the mechanism for creating strengths in operating processes which can then be exploited in many ways. Reengineering can be used to provide cost advantages or improved customer service . . . penetration of new markets . . . [and] entry into entirely new businesses either by turning internal processes into revenue-generating services or by identifying new applications for the same skills.[6]

Reengineering is a companion activity to alliance development. If one sees the reengineering process not as a downsizing methodology but rather as a reinvention of the way the business operates in order to meet the demands of a fast-changing dynamic economy, then it is clear that there is an interrelationship between alliances and reengineering. The mere process of examining an organization's capabilities will unearth opportunities for creative and innovative solutions to problems that may have become endemic to a business or even an industry. For example, the advent of on-line claims processing in the insurance and health-care industries has redesigned a work process that has been cumbersome into one that accelerates response time and cash flow for payees.

As with strategic alliance development, successful reengineering requires a commitment that is organizationwide and comes from the top. It also causes stress. New work processes may require retraining, downsizing of outdated skills, and hiring of people with new capabilities. Alliance managers will constantly be improving their management processes and modifying expectations and goals. Companies that are in the latter stages of their life cycles are most often in dire need of business reengineering, yet the further along in the stages of the life cycle a company is, the more difficult it will be to gain internal approval. In many instances, these companies and their managers don't even see the corporate, individual managerial, or project personalities as issues that could dramatically affect the success of an alliance.

Often, however, certain managers within a Mature or Declining company will lead the drive to examine the organization's capabilities and make appropriate changes. These remarks should not be taken to imply that entrepreneurial companies have no need of the reengineering process. Business reengineering may have to become a part of innovative companies' culture if they are to keep ahead of competitors.

For companies that have examined their skill base in the core competency analysis, a myriad of opportunities will become clear for applications of existing competencies, or outsourcing of non-core skills. The business processes can be discovered through reengineering. The philosophy of how to apply those processes then moves into alliance strategy development and implementation. The activities are mutually supportive and complementary.

Conclusion: The Alliance Manager for the Twenty-first Century

In this chapter, we've looked at some of the macro issues of which future-oriented managers must be aware, so that they can evaluate alliance-management decisions and risks in a broader context. Such a manager will look at the economic and political trends and ensure that his company's alliances fit within that larger picture.

He will also ask questions that encourage the organization to put the normal modus operandi aside in order to examine options and alternatives, questions such as, Is ours a company that always acquires, or should we limit our investment and expand our local access by allying with a local partner? Do we have a strategy that looks at economic as well as industry cycles, or should we discuss developing one?

The successful alliance manager will also examine the real meaning of globalism to his own company as well as that of his partner, in order to avoid pitfalls in communication. He will consider the management movement toward virtuality rather than vertical integration, and this requires that he first understand his organization's core competencies.

Finally, the manager with a macro perspective will also consider whether the team designing and managing the alliance includes "new" managers for the millennium, with local skills for managing the sensitive micro issues as well as the intricacies of cross-cultural relationships. This manager will be able to see the forest *and* the trees, and his company and its alliances will benefit accordingly.

Business is an intricate combination of variables, many of which are not within our control. The approach, methodologies, and analytical tools such as the Mindshift diagnostics described here have been designed to reduce the uncertainty in alliance development and management, and increase management capability of these challenging relationships. Thomas Edison said, "Many of life's failures are people who did not realize how close they were to success when they gave up." Don't give up on your alliances; work them harder, manage them better, and build them with more intelligence.

Appendixes

Appendixes A, B, and C are drawn from ten sessions of an executive program, "Strategic Alliances: Planning and Implementation," presented by Larraine Segil at the California Institute of Technology, Pasadena, from 1992 to 1995. This program is customized for in-company presentation through The Lared Group (see page 239).

Appendix D summarizes the results of a survey of the participants in the above program.

Appendix A:
Participant Companies in the Seminar "Strategic Alliances: Planning and Implementation"

3COM
3M Company
3M Telecom Resources Division
3M Automotive Trades Division
3M Private Network Products
A.R. Wilfley & Sons
ACE Industries Textron
ADC Fibermux, Inc.
ADC Kentrox Wireless Systems
Advanced Micro Devices
Advanced Technology
  Laboratories
Aerojet, Electronic Systems
  Division
Aerojet, Propulsion Division
AIRCO
AIRCO Coating Technology
Air Products & Chemicals,
  Polymer Chemicals Division
Alldata Corporation
Allied Signal Aerospace Company
AMCC
American International
American Medical Systems, Inc.
  (Pfizer)
Ameron Pole Products Division
Amoco Production Company
Analogy
Apogee Enterprises, Inc.

Aquapore Moisture Systems, Inc.
Archive Corporation
ARCO Chemical Company
ARCO International
Armour Pharmaceutical Company
Art Center College of Design
Artisoft, Inc.
ASC Communications, Inc.
ASC Pacific, Inc.
Aspect Telecommunications
AT&T GIS NCR Microelec-
  tronics Products Division
AT&T Paradyne Corporation
Auspex Systems Inc.
Auto-Graphics, Inc.
Autosplice Inc.
Avery Dennison
B. Braun Medical Inc.
Baker Performance Chemicals
Bal Seal Engineering Company
Basic Vegetable Products
Bausch & Lomb Inc.
Baxter Diagnostics, INc.
Baxter Edwards Critical Care
  Division
Baxter Healthcare Corporation
Becton Dickinson
Bel Foods
Bio Clinic Corporation

BOC Gases
BOC Health Care
Bortec Inc.
Bridgeford Foods
BW/IP International, Inc., Fluid
  Controls Division
Cal-Shake, Inc.
CalComp, Inc., Computer
  Graphics Group
California Institute of Technology
California Instruments
  Corporation
California Microwave
Cardiometrics, Inc.
Carroll Touch, Inc.
Castelle
Centrilift, Division of Baker
  Hughes Corporation
Chase Manhattan Private Bank
Check Technology
Chevron Petroleum Technology
  Company
Chevron Research & Technology
  Company
Chiron Intraoptics
Computer Sciences Corporation
Concurrent Computer
  Corporation
Continuum Inc.
CPID, Tektronix, Inc.
Crane Company, ChemPump
  Division
CTC Corporation
Data Rentals & Sales
Datron Systems Division
Delco Electrics Corporation
Dexter Corporation
DMV Inc.
Dow Corning Corporation

Dowty Aerospace, Los Angeles
Drackett Company, The
DuPont Company
DuPont, Biotechnology Systems
DuPont Medical Products
  Department
DuPont Radiopharmaceuticals
E-Systems Inc.
E-Systems Inc., Melpar Division
Elanco Animal Health, Division
  of Eli Lilly and Company
Electric Power Research
  Institute
Electronic Arts
Envest–Southern California
  Edison
ESL Inc., Subsidiary of TRW
Exxon Chemical Company
Ferranti International Controls
FileNet Corporation
Financial Decision System, Inc.
Fleischmann's Yeast
FMC Corporation
Forethought Group, The
Fourth Shift Corporation
Freedom Communications, Inc.
Frontier Engineering, Inc.
General Research Corporation
Geothermal Surveys, Inc.
Grace Jewelers & Company
Hadco Corporation
Hallmark Cards, Inc.
Harman International
Harris Corporation
Harris Digital Telephone Systems
Heat and Control, Inc.
Heat Transfer Research, Inc.
  (HTRI)
Helisys Corporation

Herrewood Associates
Hewlett-Packard Company
HI-Port, Inc.
Hoechst Celanese
Hollister Inc.
Honeywell, Inc.
Honeywell, Micro Switch Division
Howmet Refurbishment Center
Hughes Aircraft Company
Hughes Aircraft Company, Radar
    Systems Group
Hughes, Power Control Systems
Hunt-Wesson, Inc.
IBM Corporation/J.T. Watson
    Research Center
ICI Composites, Inc.
ICI Fiberite
IMCOA
Integrated Computer Services
Integrated Systems
Interferrous, Inc.
Interhealth
Interlake, Material Handling
    Division
International Totalizator Systems,
    Inc.
Intuit
InVitro International
IOMEGA Corporation
ITT Cannon
Jorgensen Steel & Aluminum
    Company
Kabi Pharmacia Ophthalmics, Inc.
Kaiser Corporation
Kaiser Aluminum & Chemical
Kaiser Permanente
Kamen Instrumentation
Kao Infosystems Company
Key Technology, Inc.

KPBS
Kraft General Foods, KGF
    Research
Larse Corporation
Laserscope, Inc.
Laserscope and Surgical Systems
Lefiell Manufacturing Company
LNP Engineering Plastics
Lockheed Aeronautical Systems
    Company
Lockheed Corporation
Lockheed Sanders Inc.
LSI Logic Corporation
LTV Aerospace & Defense
Lunar Design, Inc.
Madge Networks Inc.
Masland Industries
Maxis
McDonnell Douglas Aerospace
    Company
Medical Infusion Technologies
Melamine Chemicals, Inc.
MGI Pharma Inc.
Micron Custom Manufacturing
    Services, Inc.
Midland-Grau, Heavy Duty
    Systems
Miles Inc., Diabetes Business
    Unit
Molding International & Engi-
    neering, Inc.
Molecular Design Ltd.
Molecular Dynamics
Monsanto Agricultural Company
Motorola
Motorola Codex
Motorola Government & Systems
    Technology Group
Motorola, GSTG

Motorola SPS/BAICD

Mountain Network Solutions, Inc.

Nalco Chemical Company

National Semiconductor Corporation

Nestlé Brand Food Service Company

NetFRAME Systems, Inc.

Network Software Associates, Inc.

Nike Inc.

No Fear

North American Chemical Company

Northern Telecom

Northrop Advanced Technology & Design Center

Northrop Commercial

Northrop Corporation

Northrop Electronics Systems Division

Northrop Grumman Corporation, B2 Division

Norton Diamond Film

Novo Nordisk Entotech, Inc.

NSP, Northern States Power Company

Nutrilite Products, Inc.

NYNEX Corporation

Octel Communications Corporation

Oki Semiconductor

Olin Corporation

Oracle Corporation

Orbital Sciences Corporation

Pacific Bell

Pacific Fluid Systems Corporation

Packard Hughes Intercontinental

PacTel Corp

Pactel Teletrac

Peritonics Medical, Inc.

Perrin Manufacturing Company

Pioneer Hi-Bred International, Inc.

Pixar

Pocino, Inc.

Praxair, Inc.

PRC Inc.

Probe Technology Corporation

Programmed Composites

Protocol Systems, Inc.

Pyramid Technology Corporation

Quebec Government Office

Rainmaker Associates

ReachAll

Reedrill, Inc.

Reliance Electric

Robinson Nugent, Inc.

Rockwell International

Rockwell International, Autonetics Strategic Systems Division

Sakura Finetek U.S.A., Inc.

Sandoz Pharmaceuticals Corporation

Scantron Corporation

Scholle Corporation

Scientific Atlanta

Security Life Reinsurance

Senco Products, Inc.

Shaklee Corporation

Shaperite Concepts Ltd.

Shell Off Shore, Inc.

Siemens Components Inc., ICD

SmithKline Beecham Clinical Laboratories

Software Publishing Corporation

South African Consul General

Southern California Edison
  Company
Sparta, Inc.
SPC Software Publishing
  Corporation
Spectradyne Inc., Spectrovision
Spectrum Holobyte, Inc.
STAC, The Data Compression
  Company
Storage Concepts
Summit Information Systems
Sunrise Medical, Bio Clinic
Sunseeds Ltd., L.P.
Syncor International Corporation
Synopsys Inc.
TA Manufacturing
Tandem Computers Inc.
Taylor Made Golf Company, Inc.
Tektronix, Inc.
Teledyne, Inc.
Teledyne Controls
Teledyne Electronic Technologies
Telos Information Systems
Texaco, U.S.A.
Thiokol Corporation
Transamerican Corporation
Transilwrap Company, Inc.
Transitions Optical, Inc.
Trident Data Systems
Tripos, Inc.

Tripos Associates
Trout Lake Farm
TRW Advanced Systems Division
Turnkey Services
Unisys Corporation
United Defense
United Defense Limited,
  Armament Systems Division
Unocal Corporation
US & Foreign Comm.
US West, Inc.
US West Communications, Inc.
USA Funds
Valent USA Corporation
Varian Associates, Inc.
View Engineering Inc.
Voice Powered Technology Inter-
  national, Inc.
Walker Richer & Quinn, Inc.
Walt Disney Company, The
Walt Disney Imagineering
  Company
Wellman, Inc.
Westec Security Inc.
Western Digital
Westec Security
White Technology, Inc.
Wisconsin Milk Marketing Board
Woodward-Clyde Consultants
Ziatech Corporation

Appendix B:
Survey Participants' Industries

Industries (self-described) of the participants in the survey conducted as part of the seminar "Strategic Alliances: Planning and Implementation." To obtain further information on the survey, see pages 239–40.

Aerospace
Aluminum
Auto Wagering, Gaming
Biotech Instrument
Cellular Telephone
Computer Manufacturing Sales
Computer Software
Controls
Data Communications
Data Processing
Defense
Defense Contractor
Defense Manufacturer
Dietary Supplements
Education
Electric Utility
Electronics
Energy
Engineering Consultants
Environmental Consulting
Ethical Pharmaceutical
Financial Services
Food
Government Communications
Hardware
Health Care

Heavy Equipment Manufacturer
Ice Cream Manufacturing
Imaging and Work Flow
Industrial Controls
Information Technology Services
Life Insurance
Lottery
Management Consulting
Manufacturing
Measurement
Measurement and Computer
Medical
Microwave Components
Military Hardware
Multimedia-Internet Color
    Printers
Newspaper, TV, Magazine
Office Products
Oil Company Division—
    Polymers
Oil Services
Packaging
Plastics
Petrochemical
Power Transmission
Process Industries

Process Automation
Radar/Processors
Rapid Prototyping
Research Equipment
Residential–Commercial–Security
Retail/Wholesale Distributor
Semiconductors

Space Hardware
Specialty Silicon Products
Sports Management
Technology Consulting
Telecommunications
Voice Recognition
Water Resources

Appendix C:
Survey Participants' Partners' Industries

Aerospace
Automotive
Computer Manufacturing, Sales
Computer Software
Electronics
Environmental Consulting
Financial Services
Hardware
Manufacturing
Materials
Medical

Multimedia-Internet
Oil Services
Packaging
Petrochemical
Process Industries
Research Equipment
Sales and Services
Semiconductors
Specialty Silicon Products
Telecommunications
Test Publishing

Appendix D:
Summary of Results
of "Strategic Alliances" Survey

Following are the key points that resulted from the survey of 235 companies who participated in the "Strategic Alliances" program.

1. Participants to the survey already had a high level of interest in alliances. They were senior executives, 85 percent male, from diverse industries; more than 50 percent of the companies represented were over $1 billion in annual revenues, but 17 percent were companies under $20 million. Partner companies were smaller: 32 percent of these were under $20 million in size and 18 percent of the partner participants were from companies $20 million to $100 million in size.

2. The vast majority of participants were in alliances of up to three years' duration with only 10 percent in alliances of more than five years.

3. The life-cycle stages and the personalities associated with them were confirmed by the participants to be valid for corporations as well as for individual managers.

4. Participants who were Politicians were less willing to diagnose their own managerial personalities as Politicians than they were their partners'. For example, where they would have classified their own managers as Farmers they classified the same personality in their partners as Politician. They were also less able to see the project personality types for their own companies, but more able to see it in their partners'. This is why it is important to have an independent facilitator to manage this diagnostic process.

5. Female participants (15 percent of total) were most likely to represent Hockeystick companies.

6. Power struggles were seen between 35 percent of alliance managers, not within their own organizations but rather with the

partner alliance managers. These struggles correlated with managerial perceptions of failure. Alliances without power struggles were more likely to be seen to be successes.

7. Ninety-eight percent of participants saw the diagnostics as important and 80 percent said knowledge of them would have specifically assisted these managers in specific ways in their alliances. Eleven percent said that the diagnostics would have greatly affected their decision to enter the alliance and 4 percent definitely would not have entered into the alliance at all if they had used the diagnostics.

8. More than half of the participants felt the personality issues in an alliance became more important over time. Seventy-three percent felt that most of the time corporate personality was a contributing factor to the lack of alliance success. Sixty-three percent attributed lack of success to individual managerial personalities, and 58 percent to project personality. Fifty-five percent of participants attributed the responsibility for lack of alliance success to the business justification.

9. The personality diagnostics were seen as more important in most cases than the business justification for perceptions of the lack of success of the alliance.

10. A partnering of medium ($20 million to $100 million) to large ($100 million to $1 billion) companies was the least likely to succeed. Large and very large (over $1 billion) would find it easier. The Hockeystick company had the greatest likelihood for success in any partnership.

11. A pairing of projects that were Bet the Farm and Market Extending had the best chance for success.

Survey Conclusions

The results of the survey show that the Mindshift personality diagnostics are a valuable tool, not only as a success enhancer but as an evaluation methodology for alliance candidate selection.

In addition, the use of the Mindshift diagnostics to analyze existing alliances and make changes for the purpose of continuous improvement can be extended and applied as a conflict-resolution mechanism.

Another conclusion is that the tools have application across many industries, and for companies of any size.

Although the use of the Mindshift diagnostics is described in this context as an alliance-improvement tool, I suggest that they are equally useful in internal issue resolution, to resolve interaffiliate and interdivisional conflict and to select the right person for a cross-functional team that has nothing to do with alliances at all. Over the five years that I have been teaching and applying these diagnostic tools, I have begun to hear these terms coming back to me in business conversation unrelated to alliances, often with executives whose company representatives have attended one of my programs. It is clear that these characterizations capture the attention of everyone—the temptation to immediately characterize yourself and those around you is compelling.

I recommend that you use the diagnostics with humor, as a facilitation and betterment tool, and not as an opportunity to attack and destroy. Their efficacy is dependent on the goodwill of the user of the mechanism, and the willingness of the receiver of the information to apply and use it for positive corporate and personal results.

A detailed survey report is available from The Lared Group (see pages 239–40).

Notes

INTRODUCTION

1. Kathryn Rudie Harrigan, *Beyond the Vision: Making Strategic Alliances Work,* keynote address at the Corporate Venturing Conference, Boston, June 1989.

CHAPTER 1. Alliances Revisited

1. See Henry Mintzberg, "The Fall and Rise of Strategic Planning," *Harvard Business Review* 72, no. 1 (January–February 1994): 108.
2. Coopers & Lybrand USA, *Trendsetter: 1993 Annual Survey of Fast-Growth Firms* (Los Angeles: Coopers & Lybrand USA, 1993), p. 1.
3. G. Steven Burrill and Stephen E. Almassy, "Electronics '93—The New Global Reality: An Industry Annual Report" (San Francisco: Ernst & Young, 1993), see pp. 19, 22.

CHAPTER 2. The Mindshift Method of Personality Diagnostics

1. The survey was used not only to gather data but also as a teaching tool and was preceded and followed by class discussion of the Mindshift personality characteristics. The didactic nature of the use of the survey could constitute a limitation of the research. Further analysis could be undertaken in which personality traits were intermingled and not identified, in a survey of executives not in a seminar environment.

CHAPTER 3. Integrating Alliances into Corporate Strategy

1. Brian Dumaine, "What's So Hot About Insiders?" *Fortune,* November 29, 1993, pp. 63–65; Mark Maremont, "Kodak's New Focus," *Business Week,* January 30, 1995, pp. 62–68.

CHAPTER 4. Corporate Self-Analysis

1. Brian Dumaine, "Why Great Companies Last," *Fortune,* January 16, 1995, p. 129.

2. Based on an interview with Denise Coley, Strategic Program Business Manager, Advanced Technology Group, Apple Computer, Inc., on January 20, 1995.

3. Pete Engardio and Gail DeGeorge, "The New Global Workplace," *Business Week* special issue "Twenty-first Century Capitalism," (June 1994), p. 28.

CHAPTER 5. Preparing for the Alliance

1. Stephen E. Weiss and William Stripp, *Negotiation with Foreign Business Persons: An Introduction for Americans with Propositions on Six Cultures* (New York: New York University Faculty of Business Administration, 1985). My material is based on the twelve-variables framework that Weiss and Shipp suggest, and I have added elements from my own experience and insights from applying the Mindshift approach.

CHAPTER 6. Cross-Cultural Alliances

1. EMF Foundation Survey, 1987, cited in Charles Hampden-Turner *Corporate Culture: From Vicious to Virtuous Circles* (London: The Economist Books Ltd., Hutchinson Business Books Ltd./Random Century Ltd., 1990), p. 39.

2. Kathryn Rudie Harrigan, *Beyond the Vision: Making Strategic Alliances Work,* keynote address at the Corporate Venturing Conference, Boston, June 1989.

3. James R. Houghton (chairman and CEO, Corning, Inc.), quoted in *Making Strategic Alliances Work: The Conference Board Report Number 1086-94-CH* (New York: The Conference Board, 1994), pp. 29–31.

4. The following material draws on articles in the *Business Week* special issue, "Twenty-first Century Capitalism" (June 1994). See Pete Engardio and Gail DeGeorge, "The New Global Workplace" and "Importing Enthusiasm," p. 122, and Neil Gross and John Carey, "In the Digital Derby There's No Inside Lane," pp. 147–48.

5. Gross and Carey, p. 152.

6. Michael R. Bonsignore (chairman and CEO of Honeywell Inc., Minneapolis), quoted in *Making Strategic Alliances Work: The Conference Board Report Number 1086-94-CH* (New York: The Conference Board, 1994), pp. 34–36.

7. Fred Young Phillips and Alice Lee, "Japanese Technology Policy: A U.S. Corporate Perspective" (Austin: IC^2 Institute, University of Texas, September 1993), Working Paper 93-09-04, pp. 17–18.

8. *Business Week,* special issue, "Twenty-first Century Capitalism." See "Capitalism: The New Model," p. 90.

9. Ibid., pp. 87–90.

10. Ibid, p. 88.

11. Geert Hofstede, *Culture's Consequences: International Differences in Work-Related Values* (Beverly Hills: Sage Publishing, 1992), see pp. 30–55.

12. EMF Foundation Survey, 1987, cited in Charles Hampden Turner, *Corporate Culture: From Vicious to Virtuous Circles,* p. 39.

13. Based on an interview with Denise Coley, Strategic Program Business Manager, Advanced Technology Group, Apple Computer, Inc., on January 20, 1995.

CHAPTER 8. A View of the Future World of Alliances

1. G. Steven Burrill and Stephen E. Almassy: "Electronics '93—The New Global Reality: An Industry Annual Report" (San Francisco: Ernst & Young, 1993), p. 37.

2. John Naisbitt, *The Global Paradox: The Bigger the World Economy the More Powerful Its Smallest Players* (New York: William Morrow, 1994), pp. 12–13, 21.

3. For a discussion of the emancipation of Asia's components producers, see Hans Katayama, "Japan's Second Wave," *Asia, Inc.,* October 1994, pp. 58–61.

4. Fumio Kodama, "Technology Fusion and the New R&D," *Harvard Business Review* 70, no. 4 (July–August 1992): 70.

5. Both citations of Professor Sterman are from John D. Sterman, *Long Wave of Decline and the Politics of Depression,* a paper presented at the Bank Credit Analysts Conference, New York, September 1992.

6. Michael Hammer, "Hammer Defends Re-Engineering," *The Economist,* November 5, 1994, p. 70.

Bibliography

BOOKS

Badaracco, Joseph. *The Knowledge Link: How Firms Compete Through Strategic Alliances.* Boston: Harvard Business School Press, 1991.

Bartlett, Christopher A., and Sumantra Ghoshal. *Managing Across Borders: The Transnational Solution.* Boston: Harvard Business School Press, 1991.

Bleeke, Joel, and David Ernst, eds. *Collaborating to Compete: Using Strategic Alliances and Acquisitions in the Global Marketplace.* New York: John Wiley & Sons, 1993.

Botkin, James W., and Jana B. Matthews. *Winning Combinations: The Coming Wave of Entrepreneurial Partnerships Between Large and Small Companies.* New York: John Wiley & Sons, 1992.

Cleland, David I., and Roland Gareis, eds. *Global Project Management Handbook.* New York: McGraw-Hill, 1994.

Collins, Timothy M., and Thomas L. Doorley, III. *Teaming Up for the 90s.* Homewood, Ill.: Business One Irwin, 1991.

Collins, Timothy M., and Thomas L. Doorley with David Connell. *Teaming Up for the 90s: A Guide to International Joint Ventures and Strategic Alliances.* New York: Deloitte & Touche, 1991.

Fiedler, Fred E., and Martin Chemers. *Improving Leadership Effectiveness: The Leader Match Concept.* 2nd ed. New York: John Wiley & Sons, 1984.

Hall, Edward T. *The Dance of Life: The Other Dimension of Time.* New York: Doubleday/Anchor Books, 1983.

Hampden-Turner, Charles. *Corporate Culture: From Vicious to Virtuous Circles.* London: The Economist Books Ltd./Hutchinson Business Books Ltd./Random Century Ltd., 1990.

Lewis, Jordan D. *Partnerships for Profit: Structuring and Managing Strategic Alliances.* New York: The Free Press, 1990.

Link, Albert N., and Laura L. Bauer. *Cooperative Research in U.S. Manufacturing: Assessing Policy Initiatives and Corporate Strategies.* Lexington, Mass.: Lexington Books, 1989.

Murphy, William J. *R&D Cooperation Among Marketplace Competitors.* New York: Quorum Books, 1991.

Naisbitt, John. *The Global Paradox: The Bigger the World Economy, the More Powerful Its Smallest Players.* New York: William Morrow, 1994.

Nevaer, Louis E. V. *Strategic Corporate Alliances: A Study of the Present, a Model for the Future.* New York: Quorum Books, 1990.

Ohmae, Kenichi. *Beyond National Borders: Reflections on Japan and the World.* Chicago: Dow Jones, 1987.

Popcorn, Faith. *The Popcorn Report: Faith Popcorn on the Future of Your Company, Your World, Your Life.* New York: Doubleday, 1991.

Starr, Martin Kenneth. *Global Corporate Alliances and the Competitive Edge: Strategies and Tactics for Management.* New York: Quorum Books, 1991.

Technology Transfer in International Business. New York: Oxford University Press, 1991.

Yip, George S. *Total Global Strategy: Managing for Worldwide Competitive Advantage.* Englewood, N.J.: Prentice-Hall, 1992.

PERIODICAL ARTICLES

Barnathan, Joyce, et al. "Bringing It All Back Home." *Business Week* Dec. 7, 1992, pp. 133–35.

Bleeke, Joel, and David Ernst. "The Way to Win in Cross-Border Alliances." *Harvard Business Review* 69, no. 6 (November–December 1991), pp. 127–35.

Byrne, John A. "The Virtual Corporation: The Company of the Future Will Be the Ultimate in Adaptability." *Business Week,* Feb. 8, 1993, pp. 98–103.

Celron, Marvin, and Owen Davies. "50 Trends Shaping the World." *The Futurist* 25, no. 5 (September–October 1991): pp. 11–21, 15.

Chan, Peng S., and Dorothy Heide. "Strategic Alliances in Technology: Key Competitive Weapon." *SAM Advanced Management Journal* 53, no. 4 (Autumn 1993): pp. 9–17.

Churbuck, David C., and Jeffrey S. Young. "The Virtual Workplace." *Forbes,* Nov. 23, 1992, pp. 184–88, 190.

Crouse, Henry J. "The Power of Partnerships." *Journal of Business Strategy* 12, no. 6 (November–December 1991), pp. 4–8.

Dyson, Esther. "Looking Backward: 2001." *Forbes,* Sept. 16, 1991, p. 178.

Green, John A. S., et al. "Strategic Partnering Aids Technology Transfer." *Research Technology Management* 34, no. 4 (July–August 1991): pp. 26–31 (Martin Marietta example).

Gyencs, Lawrence A. "Build the Foundation for a Successful Joint Venture." *Journal of Business Strategy* 13, no. 1 (November–December 1991): pp. 27–32.

Hamel, Gary. "Competition for Competence and Interpartner Learning Within International Strategic Alliances." *Strategic Management Journal* 12, no. 5/6 (July–August 1991): pp. 83–103.

Jones, Kevin K., and Walter E. Shill. "Allying for Advantage." *McKinsey Quarterly* no. 3 (1991): pp. 73–101.

Kodama, Fumio. "Technology Fusion and the New R&D." *Harvard Business Review* 70, no. 4 (July–August 1992): pp. 70–78.

Lewis, J. "Competitive Alliances Redefine Companies." *Management Review* 80, no. 4 (April 1991): p. 15.

Merrifield, Bruce. "Strategic Alliances in the Global Marketplace." *Research Technology Management* 32, no. 1 (January–February 1989): pp. 15–20.

Powell, Bill, with John Schwartz. "Good-bye, Mr. Chips: Why High-Tech Deals with Japan Could Backfire." *Newsweek,* Aug. 3, 1992, p. 60.

Rapoport, Carla. "Europe Looks Ahead to Hard Choices." *Fortune,* May 18, 1992, pp. 144–46, 148–49.

Romm, Joseph. "Japan's Flying Geese." *Forbes,* Nov. 23, 1992, pp. 108, 110–12.

Shenon, Philip. "New World Order in Asia: The U.S. Will Have to Catch Up." *New York Times,* Nov. 10, 1991, p. 87.

Sherman, Stratford. "Are Strategic Alliances Working?" *Fortune,* Sept. 21, 1992, pp. 77–78.

Smilor, Raymond W., and David V. Gibson. "Technology Transfer in Multi-Organizational Environments: The Case of R&D Consortia." *IEEE Transactions on Engineering Management* 38, no. 1 (February 1991): pp. 3–13.

Sterman, John D. *Long Wave Decline and the Politics of Depression.* Paper presented at the Bank Credit Analyst Conference, New York, September 17, 1992.

Electronic Business, special issue, March 30, 1992, "Strategic Alliances: 3rd Annual CEO Survey." See Stephen E. Almassy, "A New Mind-set for Electronics Executives," p. 83; Peter Burrows, "How a Good Partnership Goes Bad," pp. 86–88, 90; E. B. Baatz, "Better Together: Big Blue and Little Easel," pp. 103–4; Tom Peters, "Perception Is All There Is," p. 106; Barbara Jorgensen, "Mercedes-Benz and Bose Thought They Knew Everything. Surprise!" pp. 113–14; David Webb, "A Buyer-

Supplier Alliance That Really Works," pp. 137–38; E. B. Baatz, "Words from on High," pp. 145–47; L. Scott Flaig, "The Virtual Enterprise: Your New Model for Success," pp. 153–55.

Treece, James B. "The Partners." *Business Week,* Feb. 10, 1992, pp. 102–7.

Venkatesan, Ravi. "Strategic Sourcing: To Make or Not To Make." *Harvard Business Review* 70, no. 6 (November–December 1992): pp. 98–107.

Zachary, G. Pascal, "High-Tech Firms Find It's Good to Line Up Outside Contractors." *Wall Street Journal,* July 29, 1992, p. A6.

Author's Note

You are invited to contact the author with your questions, comments, and experiences in applying the concepts in this book to your own organization or to obtain further information on the following seminars:

- **Managing Globally: Building Global Competency for Executives**
- **Post Merger and Acquisition Strategies**
- **Strategic Alliances**
- **Strategic Planning**
- **The Mindshift Method**
- **Other programs available from Larraine Segil and The Lared Group**

The following materials are available:

- Copyrighted forms and charts from this book on IBM Compatible Windows, Word for Windows, and/or Powerpoint. $15 per copy.
- Two additional case studies that are useful for group discussion and workshops. $50 each.
- The Mindshift Questionnaire, the most convenient tool for diagnosing corporate, managerial, and project personalities. $10 per copy.
- The Mindshift Survey: Results of four years of research undertaken by the author within the framework of her "Strategic Alliances" program presented at the California Institute of

Technology Industrial Relations Center, on the alliance activities of the program's 235 participant companies. $10 per copy.

Please provide phone, fax, and E-mail information with your address, and send a Federal Express or UPS billing number with your check.

The author also offers statistical analysis of completed Mindshift Questionnaires, along with an interpretation of the data and evaluative report. Please inquire for further details.

Address correspondence to:

Larraine Segil, Partner,
The Lared Group
1901 Avenue of the Stars
Suite 280
Los Angeles, CA 90067

Tel: (310) 556–1778
Fax: (310) 556–8085
E-mail: Lsegil@aol.com

Index

Note: ⋆ = name changed in text